# Rudolf Steiner's Esoteric Christianity

# in the Grail painting by Anna May

Adrian Anderson  Ph.D.

Contemplating the sacred in Rosicrucian Christianity

Threshold Publishing, Australia  2017
www.rudolfsteinerstudies.com

Distributed by Ebook Alchemy P/L
Prahran East
VIC  3198
Australia

© 2017  A. Anderson     Revised edition 2021

The author asserts the moral right to be regarded as the originator of this book

ISBN  978-0-9941602-7-0  paperback
ISBN  978-0-9941602-8-7  hardback

# Contents

**Foreword** — 2

**Introduction**: About Anna May: the background to the painting — 5

**The Left Side** — 8
Melchizedek / Abraham-Isaac & Jacob / King Solomon, Hiram, the Queen of Sheba / King Solomon & Hiram Abiff / Solomon's temple / The Queen of Sheba with King Solomon & Hiram / The High Priest's breastplate / The Queen of Sheba & the Spirit-self / Hail to the Jewel in the Lotus ! / the Veil before the Holy of Holies / The Zodiac Ages involved here

**The Left Side, below** — 27
Moses, the burning bush and the Menorah / Understanding the "I am the I am" / The two horns of Moses / The Menorah-bush / The zodiac under the menorah / Gemini and Zarathustra / The images in the zodiac / Capricorn and the energy lines / The Ark of the Covenant / The Angels of the pre-Golgotha Mysteries

**The Middle Section** — 36
Jachin and Boaz / The two columns in the painting / The left column & the Egyptian Time-Spirit / the right column & the Greek Time-spirit / Novalis: Hymn to the Night / The World-Cross: Plato and the enchanted Deity / Rudolf Steiner & the World-Cross / The Crucifixion Scene / Christ as the Spirit of the Earth / A crowd of witnesses / The Subterranean world / Joseph of Arimathea / The Holy Grail
The Two Columns within the human being /
Initiatory secrets: Joseph of Arimathea or the Earth-soul ?

**The Middle Section, above** — 59
The legend of the Cross / A new Tree of Life / The Pentagram / the Ouroboros / The Son of Man / Alchemy: an over-view / The legend of "The Stone of the Wise Men and the Child Jesus" / The Philosopher's Stone / Initiatory secrets in the Greek New Testament / The Three, the Twelve and the Four / The burdened Archangels / Archangel Michael versus Lucifer 3,000 BC

**The Right side**     70
Archangel Gabriel / AD 1250: the initiation of Christian Rosencreutz /
The Dove & the Holy Spirit / Royal Arch Freemasonry /
The cosmic forces operative in the year AD 1250 / The tetramorph pedestal /
The influence of Taurus / The 'diamond body' / The group around the sarcophagus

**The Lower Right Side**     83
On the road to Damascus: The Holy of Holies /
The Ascending dove / The Subdued Bull forces / The Heruben Papyrus /
St. Paul encounters the Risen Christ / The new Holy of Holies within: the Saviour
and the eternal "I am" / The nature of Jesus Christ in anthroposophy /
The World Saviour / The Holy Grail / The Etheric Reappearing of Christ Jesus /
The sacred revelation from Rudolf Steiner about the response of Christ Jesus
to being tormented and crucified /
A report of an encounter with Christ Jesus in the ether /
The Zodiac beneath the bush of seven roses / The Fall of Lucifer /
The Sophia woman of the Apocalypse / Michael and the Dragon /

**Conclusion**     107

**Appendix**
**1: The Description written by Anna May in 1918**     108

**2: More about the name of God spoken to Moses**     110
   God's name: "I am that I am" (ehyeh asher ehyeh) / the eternal "I" /
   the initiatory meaning of 'ehyeh asher ehyeh' /

**3: Photo of the 1918 large different version**, from the Munich exhibition     115

**Glossary**     116
**Index**     118

Other books by the author
Author's website & how to obtain a copy of this painting
Illustration acknowledgements

**Illustrations** page

1 The entire painting — 1
2 Anna May and the Glass Palace — 3
3 Typical landscape paintings by Anna May — 6
4 Melchizedek — 9
5 King Solomon, Queen of Sheba and Hiram — 13
6 A diagram of King Solomon's Temple — 16
7 *Queen of Sheba meeting king Solomon*, by E. Poytner — 19
8 The *Mons Philosophorum*, a Rosicrucian diagram — 24
9 Two lines over to the Armillary sphere in the Piscean Age — 26
10 Moses kneeling before the burning-bush-menorah — 28
11 The zodiac — 31
12 The Ark and Angels — 34
13 The left column - Time-Spirit — 38
14 The right column - Time-Spirit — 39
15 Cultural identifiers for Pharao and Hellas — 40
16 The Crucifixion scene — 45
17 The Subterranean figures — 49
18 Upper part of the Tree of Life — 58
19 The Archangels, left and right sides — 69
20 The 'burdened' Archangels Michael and Gabriel — 71
21 Initiation scene in AD 1250 — 74
22 A Royal Arch tracing board — 77
23 Identifying the persons of AD 1250 — 82
24 The Ascent of the Dove, and the bull — 84
25 The Heruben Papyrus from ancient Egypt — 87
26 St. Paul, Christ and the seven-rose menorah — 91
27 A Masonic zodiac — 98
28 The Fall of Lucifer — 101
29 The Sophia-soul of the Apocalypse — 102
30 Archangel Michael enchaining the Dragon — 105

**1 The Triptych Grail:** designed by Rudolf Steiner, painted by Anna May in 1912. (size was approx. 2.5 m in length) A colour slide, made about 1912, survived the war and from this an art print was made in 1975.

## Foreword

Rudolf Steiner (1861-1925) provided the world with an unprecedented body of wisdom about important spiritual life-questions covering a very wide range of themes. These are published in some 360 books, and in addition, his work includes: about 100 paintings or drawings, 14 buildings designed in a new organic architectural style, many hundreds of choreographic forms for the new art of movement called eurythmy. In addition, there is the profound pedagogical advice which gave rise to the Steiner schools, as well as pharmaceutical formulae used in anthroposophical medicine, and the practical indications for organic farming which led to bio-dynamic agriculture. His high initiation consciousness allowed him to understand and to teach a profound, cosmic aspect to Christ and the role of various initiates historically in serving the Christ-Impulse. This contribution of Rudolf Steiner resulted in an esoteric Christianity which the world had never before experienced.

The most esoteric work of art ever created through the initiative of Rudolf Steiner is a painting from about 1912, known as the *Triptych Grail*, which depicts many sacred truths of esoteric Christianity. This magnificent work of art, about 2.5 metres in length, is fading from memory today, and yet it is reported, by her niece, Margaretha Hauschka, that Rudolf Steiner intended this painting to be placed inside the Goetheanum for future generations to experience. So it is my hope that through this book, and through making quality reproductions of this painting available, this sacred artwork can live on in the hearts of future generations.

This large artwork was painted by the gifted German artist, Anna May (1864-1954), who was trained by the widely respected Professor Nikolaus Gysis, and who was later married to Thaddeus von Rychter, a painter well-known in Germany, especially in Munich art circles. Rudolf Steiner also regarded her artwork highly, and gave her various artistic tasks, after the completion of the great *Triptych Grail* painting. Her niece, Margaretha Hauschka, reported in the weekly Anthroposophical Society newsletter, *Das Goetheanum*, Anna May received many tasks from Rudolf Steiner. For example, she painted a picture to illustrate the theme of the meditative verse given during a lecture in 1914. This painting was then published in advance, in a format of 12 x 20 cm, with a hand-written copy of the verse included. When members of the Anthroposophical Society took their seats for this lecture of 26. Dec. 1914, they found placed on their seats, a copy of this art print. It was also arranged for this art print to be sent to soldiers in the battlefield as a Christmas gift.[1]

> In the eye of the soul is reflected the Earth's radiant hope,
> Wisdom, devoted to the spirit, in human hearts speaks thus:
> The Father's eternal Love did send the Son to the Earth,
> who, full of Grace, now bestows on humanity's pathway, the radiance of Heaven.

Anna May gave her great painting the title, "*The Triptych Grail: from Solomon across Golgotha to Christian Rosencreutz*". She referred to this artwork as a 'sketch' because later she painted a larger, but quite different version of it. In 1975, late in her life, Hauschka made available for purchase a poster of the original painting, the sketch. This poster was made from the glass-plate photograph taken of the painting. Sometime before 1918, Anna May painted a different, much larger version of the painting, which lacks the quality of the original painting. This new version was exhibited in the famous Munich Crystal Palace in 1918, between July and September. A photograph of this larger painting were included in the Exhibition catalogue (see Appendix 3 for this image). This larger, decidedly inferior version was also put on exhibition in a private anthroposophical gallery, *Das Reich*, in Munich; this version was photographed in three sections, and these three images were recorded in the Catalogue for this gallery. A copy of the original Catalogue is kept in the Goetheanum library.

Apart from the glass-plate photograph of the sketch, Hauschka also published a two page folded pamphlet about the Triptych Grail painting, to be provided with the poster. See Appendix 1 for a

---

[1] Extracted from Irmgard Marbach's, "*Margareth Hauschka Ein Lebensbild*", Margarethe Hauschka-Schule, 1995, 73087 Boll über Göppingen, Gruibinger Straße 29.

**2 Anna May**; photo taken in the years after the loss of her husband, Thaddeus Rychter, in Poland, in 1939.

The Glass Palace in Munich, where a version of part of the painting was exhibited in 1918.

translation of this pamphlet, which gives a brief overview of the themes, and identifies many of the persons and spiritual beings depicted. The huge later painting, some 6 metres long, was eventually placed in the Hamburg Steiner School. Hauschka writes, "*It was a painting that filled an entire wall, the size of which I estimated was 2.5 to 3 metres high and 6 metres long*".[2] In the 1940's, this school, together with this painting, was destroyed during the fire-storms created by Allied bombings. What happened to the magnificent, original 2.5m painting is unknown. But it is very fortunate for people interested in deeper spiritual understanding of Christianity, that a colour photograph taken of this original 'sketch', by the mother of Margaretha Hauschka, and later made available as a poster, survived the wars in Europe. The artwork presented in this book is the result of scanning a reproduction which was made from the poster.

This image has been very carefully enhanced, and compared to the glass-plate photograph from 1912,[3] to clarify as many of the details as possible, and allow the viewer to see the fantastical array of divine beings, spiritual energies and human beings that it portrays – without altering any of its details. During this work, some details remained slightly blurred or faded, since the camera lens could not possibly register in full clarity all of the intricate details in such a large painting. In keeping with what is such an esoteric work of art, Rudolf Steiner advised Anna May that when the painting was complete, it would need a very special kind of frame. As Margueritha Hauschka reports it should be,

> A broad frame of wood, somewhat arched and vault-like. Below, it should have a kind of ledge, like a broad altar. The entire wooden frame itself should be bright and lustrous, but with an indigo-blue stain. In the arch above, the zodiac should be depicted, the constellations however, lightly enveloped, with the images depicted there like a golden mist, in which the stars shine forth.

Just what zodiac images Rudolf Steiner intended for this frame, is unknown. It could be traditional zodiac imagery, or it could be the images that were being painted onto the ceiling of the Centre in Stuttgart, at this same time. These images, and the entire building, were destroyed in 1937; but they are available again in my book, *The Lost Zodiac of Rudolf Steiner*.

With regard to clarifying some of the details of the 100-year old image, I carried out further work on them, to enhance their visibility, taking particular care not to actually change any image. There are also some details which only became visible when parts of the painting were examined under a magnification, or when its colours were given more contrast than the dark background, on a computer. The few instances where I have enhanced a detail shall be clearly identified as we explore the painting.

---

[2] From "Das Goetheanum", the weekly publication from Dornach, 15th.June 1975.
[3] Due to the kindness of Herr Norbert Reininger, I was able to see a copy of the original glass plate photograph.

# Introduction

In the years prior to the First World War, Rudolf Steiner's extraordinary activity was flourishing in many areas of the spiritual and cultural life of Europe. His popularity was growing strongly and his lectures and conferences embraced both esoteric truths about the spiritual path, the role of initiates in humanity's history, an esoteric understanding of Christianity, and also the Arts. Artists such as Piet Mondrian, Thaddeus von Rychter and Kandinsky came to hear him speak on a new understanding of the language of colour.

Anna May was a friend of Thaddeus von Rychter and through him she met Rudolf Steiner in 1911 and quickly became deeply devoted to his teachings; despite strong opposition from her family. Thaddeus von Rychter later became her life partner. In 1911 and 1912, Rudolf Steiner's lectures, which were attended by Anna May, were often about esoteric Christianity, and therefore about the great initiate Christian Rosencreutz. Rudolf Steiner's unique insights into the esoteric truths and existential significance of the Christ reality resulted in the imminent need to split from the Theosophical Society, with its emphasis on eastern wisdom, and to form the Anthroposophical Society, wherein deeply esoteric Christian truths would be welcome. Shortly after becoming a student of Rudolf Steiner in 1911, inspired by his revelations concerning the Rosicrucian-Christian impulse, and after some discussion with him, Anna May began work on this painting.

Around 1911, Rudolf Steiner spoke with Anna May, giving her guidance about the overall theme and appearance of the painting.[4] But how did the artist actually succeed in creating accurately such a complex painting? There are many esoteric details in it, and some 54 specific persons or spirit beings, not including the crowd of some 20 witnesses, near the Cross. The answer to this question can be found in a letter which Anna May wrote from Palestine to a friend, about the years 1911-12, when she first encountered anthroposophy and was inspired to create this painting. As she later wrote to this friend,

> My family could not understand that for me {through encountering anthroposophy} a new life-energy flowed into me, a situation which felt wonderful to me, for I was by now at an age where to me emptiness in Art allowed feelings to creep in whereby the days became dreary. The most wonderful thing that I encountered in my life occurred, when at night-time, for months, as everyone else was asleep, I arose and brought all that I had acquired recently {through becoming acquainted with Rudolf Steiner's teachings} into a large painting.
>
> Section after section of this painting appeared before me, in a manner which I have never experienced again; **these parts appeared as if being whispered to me**. And, later {in the night} as I lay down again, towards sunrise, **then there appeared the most unexpected images before my closed eyes**... the 'threads' of this painting never were broken; they entwined themselves tenaciously through all of my day's activities and conversations. The people who were around daily **could not interfere with my being focused on this**. A blessedness enveloped me, which was all the greater, as I had already given up hope of finding something of interest in life.[5]     (emphasis mine, A.A.)

This large and very complex painting came into being successfully, as a spiritual blessing from Rudolf Steiner. Its many details were kept clearly before the painter's soul day and night. Because she kept seeing the images over many months, she could complete the difficult task of actually painting not only many complex details, but also thereby depict such profound secrets of esoteric Christianity. As she herself indicates in the letter, the details were unexpected to her, so she was not 'working out' the details; rather, they were bestowed upon her. After Anna May migrated to Jerusalem, she worked as a painter into her eighties, but none of her other paintings

---

[4] From a report in *Das Goetheanum*, 1975, no. 24.
[5] Extracted from Irmgard Marbach, "*Margareth Hauschka Ein Lebensbild*", Margarethe Hauschka-Schule.

**3 Other paintings by Anna May-Rychter** during her many years in Jerusalem.

She painted watercolour street scenes and landscapes.

Top: Capernaum

Middle: Arabs in Jerusalem gathered around for coffee.

Below: A view of Jerusalem.

These paintings kindly made available by the Antiques dealer who owns them: (Ivanantiques)

deal with such esoteric themes as this exceptional highly esoteric work; she painted scenes of life around the Holy Lands, see Illustration 3. In 1924, she settled in Jerusalem where she earned a very modest living as a painter. She experienced the tragedy of her husband, Thaddeus Rychter, sailing back to Europe in 1939, to carry out an artistic commission in Poland, never to return. He died somewhere in Poland in the war, and his body was never found. Anna herself lived on until 1954. She was held in such high regard by all who knew her, because of her spirituality inspired by her understanding of esoteric Christianity, that a local newspaper article reported her death with the words, "Jerusalem's last saint has died".

**Overview of the painting *The Triptych Grail***
It presents many sacred initiation truths of the Christ-Mysteries, but in particular it has the theme of the striving over lifetimes, of the great initiate known as Christian Rosencreutz, from whom the Rosicrucian impulse arose in the Middle Ages. It also has elements of deep truths indicated in Biblical teachings, some of which are a focus in Freemasonry. It also incorporates features about the mysterious Holy Grail and alchemy. It culminates in a presentation of the holiest of the truths in anthroposophy: those which concern the link between the individual human being and Christ Jesus. It starts at the left side, with core dynamics and beings of the past, and it ends on the far right with spiritual beings and dynamics that lie in the future. We shall start in a vertical area at the far left of the painting, which has Melchizedek depicted at the top; see illustration 4.

This is the only image from Rudolf Steiner depicting this mysterious and deeply revered being. In the dark area below him, there is, as Anna May reported, the great patriarch Abraham with his son Isaac (unfortunately neither of them could be made any clearer). Below these two people, quite visible, is Jacob when having his famous dream about a ladder going up to heaven, (see below for more about these two people).

# The left side

## Melchizedek

The figure wearing a prominent ceremonial head-dress in a golden colour is Melchizedek. He is enveloped in streams of energy, mainly in shades of gold. It appears that these energy-streams flowing around this great being come from a source above him, which fade out to his left, near to a spiritual being whose face is faintly visible, see illustration 4. The source of the energy lines sweeping around this great spiritual being is very likely the spiritual-sun. The face of Melchizedek seems to have a slightly Asian appearance. So, who is this being, and what is his role here?

In the book of Genesis, chapter 14, the mysterious being Melchizedek is mentioned, and in a very significant connection. He is presented as that entity who inaugurates the tremendous mission of Abraham, which was to establish the twelve tribes of Israel. That is, to begin the lineage of the twelve Hebrew tribes who were destined to be the ancestors of Jesus, the man who would be the vessel of the descending Sun God. Without this involvement of Abraham there would have been, in effect, no Mystery of Golgotha, as the ancient Hebrew nation would not have come into being. The passage in Genesis occurs whilst relating the battles with chieftains of opposing Semitic tribes that Abraham was involved in, as he attempted to gain control of the promised land.

> Verses 15-17: During the night Abram divided his men to attack them and he routed them, pursuing them as far as Hobah, north of Damascus. He recovered all the goods and brought back his relative Lot and his possessions, together with the women and the other people. After Abram returned from defeating Kedorlaomer and the kings allied with him, the king of Sodom came out to meet him in the Valley of Shaveh {that is, the King's Valley}.
> Verses 18-20: Then Melchizedek, king of Salem brought out bread and wine. He was a priest of God Most High, and he blessed Abram, saying, "Blessed be Abram by God Most High, Creator of heaven and earth. And blessed be God Most High, who delivered your enemies into your hands." (Gen:14)

This encounter has of course triggered off enormous interest in students of the Bible, since many people conclude that Melchizedek is a higher person (or being) than Abraham. Theologians query the account of this event, because it is so striking; some have concluded that it is a later insertion into the story of Abraham, and just doesn't have any validity. This is because there is firstly, the confronting idea that the mission of the great Patriarch is given to him by a mysterious person who refers to a deity, "God Most High" who was worshipped by the Canaanites.

But in addition, there are several astonishing elements to the nature of Melchizedek, mentioned elsewhere in the Bible, which add to his mystique. In Psalm 110, an important and complex reference is made to Melchizedek when the nature of the coming Messiah is being mentioned. It appears to be referring to the future Day of Pentecost, when the first disciples receive from Christ the Holy Spirit (and thus also to some extent, a future time when the redeemed humanity unites with Christ). There are also some Psalms which have profound esoteric meanings, whilst others refer to historical realities, such as the struggle of king David and the later Hebrew priesthood to maintain Israel. Psalm 110 is a psalm which contains a deeply esoteric message which reflects initiatory wisdom, but is written in ambiguous Hebrew. A section of Psalm 110 lines can be translated as follows:

> Thy people shall offer themselves freely,
> beautiful in raiments of holiness,
> on the Day of thy Empowerment.
> Thou shalt receive thy disciples like dew,

**4 Melchizedek:** the great leader of the Atlantean Sun Oracle.

> from the womb of the morning.
> For the Lord has sworn,
> and will not waver,
> Thou art a priest in the Order of Melchizedek forever.

So here the future Messiah is described as having a role in the cosmos similar to that of Melchizedek. The other intriguing reference is from the New Testament, the Epistle of the Hebrews,

> ….Without father or mother, without genealogy,
> without beginning of days or end of life,
> like the Son of God he remains a priest forever. (Heb 7:3)

Here is an unusual description of this being, Melchizedek – especially that is, if one assumes that he is a human being. In theological circles, to resolve this mystery, two different views formed. One view is that it is simply the case that the parents of this human being were not listed in any ancestral list. This (incorrect) view has been actually embedded in the Peshitta Bible or old Aramaic version of the New Testament, by changing the correct Greek text (in Hebrews 7:3) to incorrectly read, "whose mother and father are not listed in any genealogies". The other view, held by the great Alexandrian church father, Origenes, (and a variety of Gnostics) is the more accurate one, and is in general harmony with Rudolf Steiner's research. Namely, that these words about him having no lineage, are meant to indicate that Melchizedek is not a human being, but a spiritual being.

Rudolf Steiner reveals in various ways that Melchizedek was a spirit being. He verifies and (partially) explains this nature by revealing that an ancient esoteric Coptic text about Christ is quite correct when it records in a deeply esoteric and strangely evocative statement, that "Melchizedek is the Light-purifier before Christ". That is, the spirit being whose task it was to ensure that the etheric and astral radiance from the sun-sphere, streaming down to the Earth's aura was not tainted by malignant influences.[6] Hence there is real initiation wisdom in the Psalmist's words when he says "…. the LORD {JHVH} has sworn and will not change his mind: "You are a priest forever, in the Order of Melchizedek". (Ps. 110:4) This is indicating that Jesus Christ is "in the Order of Melchizedek", meaning he belongs to that rank of being, in general terms.

The term used three times in Genesis, "God Most High" (in Hebrew, El-Elyon) which occurs 28 times in the Scriptures is of course, different to the usual name for God in the Old Testament, "JHVH", which is often spoken and written as 'Jahweh'. This term, "God Most High", is understood in normal, exoteric studies as a highly reverential way of addressing God (JHVH). But in the light of Rudolf Steiner's comments, El-Elyon can be understood as referring to a higher divine reality than the one Elohim or 'Spirit of Form', called JHVH. It refers to all of these divine beings, and in particular to the highest of the Elohim or Spirits of Form, the cosmic Christ. We can call these beings 'sun gods'; and the highest of these beings, the Powers, is the cosmic Christ.

This allows one to realize that the references to Melchizedek form a rare instance of a spiritual being, a leader of initiates, having a role in the Bible. But it also becomes clear that Melchizedek is therefore a being closely associated with the cosmic Christ. Rudolf Steiner reveals that Melchizedek was the spiritual being who led the Sun Mysteries in Atlantean times, the highest of the initiatory temples of that era. The Oracles or Mystery temples in that age (and on into ancient Egyptian times) were led by Angelic beings, and in one lecture Rudolf Steiner describes Melchizedek as "one aeon ahead of humanity", which is a way of describing the Angels. Rudolf Steiner explains that,

> Melchizedek had the task in the Atlantean Age to research, together with his helpers, {the initiated priests in the Sun Oracle of Atlantis} the spiritual existence of the Sun itself.

---

[6] GA 95 p. 156.

> Thus he had as his task to teach all the secrets of the planets and the sun {the planetary-solar system}. [7]

Rudolf Steiner describes the significance of the meeting of Abraham and Melchizedek in these words, "This meeting of Abraham with Melchizedek is a meeting of the greatest, most universal significance...he communicated to Abraham the secret of the Sun sphere..."[8] About this meeting, we need to be aware that it was a clairvoyant experience of a very unusual kind. Rudolf Steiner's words about this meeting are, "in order not to bewilder Abraham, Melchizedek showed himself in the etheric body of Shem".[9] Shem was a son of Noah, and he would have had a Semitic appearance, so Melchizedek in using the etheric body of Shem, thereby could make his appearance more understandable (less alienating) to Abraham. One gains the impression that the meeting involved Abraham being given some etheric clairvoyance, and not realizing that he was interacting with a divine being clad within an etheric body, because an etheric body can condense itself so as to appear very like a physical reality to an observer. It is significant that the mystical Jewish traditions since at least the first century AD have identified Melchizedek with Shem.[10] This appears to reflect some knowledge of this esoteric secret in Judaism.

Rudolf Steiner explains that when Melchizedek brought bread and wine to Abraham, it was not simply refreshments, but a sacrament anticipating the ritual use of bread and wine which would be used by Christ in the Last Supper. This sacrament has various purposes to it; is about sanctifying daily life for a no-longer-directly-clairvoyant people, by pragmatically linking daily life, especially nutrition through fluid and solid matter, to the Divine. It would also in this way subtly speak to the Hebrews, and later to Christians, of the sins that they would need help with from the Divine. But the underlying perspective here is, as Rudolf Steiner explained, since a sin arises when one is incarnate, and hence consuming earthly substances, it would only be in the course of future lives that atonement for such imperfections could be attained, helping free oneself from the karma, and also helping to heal the Earth.

Understood in this way, one realizes that this ritual, established most likely in 1846 BC, is also signifying that Melchizedek was a forerunner to Christ.[11] This is true in various ways, and here there is a subtle link as Rudolf Steiner explained, when Christ - who would re-institute the ritual of bread and wine - healed someone in his lifetime, saying that his or her sins "were forgiven". For in saying this, Christ was aware that the karmic burden of that person's past misdeed had now run its course. (Rudolf Steiner's lectures on the Gospel of St. Matthew are essential reading here.)

Rudolf Steiner describes Melchizedek as an Angelic being, and not a human being. In one lecture he calls him, "the Angel of the 'earthly rotation time' {cycles}"; in another he is described as being the "Light-purifier {for the earthly world} prior to the cosmic Christ taking on this task {after the events of Golgotha".[12]

In the painting by Anna May this being seems to have an Asian appearance; this reflects Rudolf Steiner's research that, amongst the various ethnicities in the world today, the Asian people have an appearance most like that of the Atlantean peoples. Not that Melchizedek was an incarnate human being, but he would have been active amongst his students, through a human being. This was the usual dynamic with the high angelic beings who exerted their influence in human culture via the priests or the king. This situation is important to realize, as it explains the otherwise confusing statement from Rudolf Steiner that Melchizedek was Noah, who selected Atlanteans

---

[7] GA 109/11, ps. 41, 44.
[8] GA 123, p.78.
[9] GA 123. *The Gospel of St. Matthew*, lecture 4th Sept. 1910.
[10] This is found for example in the Targums (Neofiti 1).
[11] To read more about the cosmic timing of the Melchizedek-Abraham event, and the link between it and the arising of Rudolf Steiner's work, see my book, *Rudolf Steiner's Lost Zodiac*.
[12] In GA 89, p. 241 (German edition), lecture of 2nd July 1904, and in GA 95, p. 157, Question & Answer session.

and led them out of Atlantis before it was destroyed. Noah was presumably a physical person, to whom Melchizedek was able to make his intentions known.

So the painting, which is in essence about the initiates and the 'Christ-Mystery' or the sun-god Christ, starts appropriately with an image of this spiritual leader of the ancient initiation centre of Atlantis. This centre was the temple of the Sun Oracle, dedicated to the sun-god, whom we understand to be the cosmic Christ. Underneath Melchizedek is Abraham, with his son Isaac and his grandson Jacob; but in the painting we can only see a glimpse of Abraham and nothing of Isaac.

**Abraham, Isaac and Jacob**
We have already mentioned the main significance of Abraham, but we have noted that Anna May reports that he is depicted with his son, Isaac. The inclusion of Isaac here points to two themes; one is the high level of obedience and self-sacrifice which was required of those who are servants of divine will. The other theme is that of the importance of the zodiac to the Biblical message. The theme of serving divine will, of being obedient to higher powers, is referring to Abraham's crucial spiritual test. This test involved being (apparently) ordered to sacrifice his son to God; this is described in Genesis, chapter 22. The Bible narrative reports that, as a result of his obedience, Isaac is 'restored' to Abraham, that is, he is exempted from being a sacrifice. In this way, the great mission of Abraham, through his son Isaac, is established, as a reward from God. Rudolf Steiner explains that this episode, so alien to us today, has to do with the stern requirement of a servant of Jehovah to manifest the greatest possible surrender of his own will.[13] Hence the apparent call to sacrifice his son.

The zodiac theme is discreetly presented here, because the descendants of Abraham, the twelve tribes of Israel, were a reflection of the zodiac forces. In Genesis, 26:4, the declaration was made by God to Abraham, "For I shall make your descendants to multiply like the stars of heaven". Rudolf Steiner explains that "like the stars of heaven" actually means, "in accordance with the twelve constellations of the zodiac".[14] The zodiac plays an important underlying role in this painting; it is depicted at least three times. The twelve tribes derive from the sons of Jacob, the grandson of Abraham. The painting depicts Jacob, in the bottom left-hand corner at a crucial time in his life, at the place called Bethel. As Genesis describes (chapter 28) Jacob has a spiritual experience there, wherein he sees a kind of ladder reaching up to heaven, and divine beings ascending and descending on this ladder. Then God appears and tells him that in effect, he is to become the founder of Israel,

> Ge 28:10 Jacob left Beersheba and set out for Haran. Ge 28:11 When he reached a certain place,[i] he stopped for the night because the sun had set. Taking one of the stones there, he put it under his head and lay down to sleep. Ge 28:12 He had a dream in which he saw a stairway resting on the earth, with its top reaching to heaven, and the angels of God were ascending and descending on it. Ge 28:13 There above it stood the LORD, and he said: "I am the LORD, the God of your father Abraham and the God of Isaac. I will give you and your descendants the land on which you are lying. Ge 28:14 Your descendants will be like the dust of the earth, and you will spread out to the west and to the east, to the north and to the south. All peoples on earth will be blessed through you and your offspring.

Obviously the purpose behind the founding of Israel was to bring the Messiah into the world.

---

[13] GA 117, 9th Nov. & 19th Nov. 1909.
[14] For more about the mission of Abraham and the connection of this to Rudolf Steiner, see my book *The Lost Zodiac of Rudolf Steiner*.

5 King Solomon, the Queen of Sheba and Hiram inside the Temple

### King Solomon, Hiram and the Queen of Sheba

We shall now explore the scene immediately to the right of Abraham, which shows three persons, mentioned in the Bible, persons who are also very prominent in Freemasonry. Rudolf Steiner had commenced leading a group of theosophists in an unorthodox form of Freemasonry, known as the Rites of Memphis and Mizraim, or Egyptian Freemasonry. The inclusion of Freemasonry elements in the painting has several purposes. Firstly, the lives of the holy high initiate Christian Rosencreutz are a major theme in this painting. In careful, non-sensational words, Rudolf Steiner revealed to a small group of serious students, that Christian Rosencreutz had been Hiram the master builder, in a past life.

> The individuality of Hiram was re-born in the time when the great sun-spirit, the Christ, lived in Jesus of Nazareth...Christ Jesus placed the seeds of new life in his heart. Lazaros was new-awakened to the spiritual existence, new-born as the disciple 'whom Jesus loved'.[15]

This means that the great leader of the Rosicrucian movement has been involved in an esoteric activity that would later become a central part of the Masonic tradition. (After the Golgotha events, Jesus Christ is often referred to as 'Christ Jesus" by Rudolf Steiner.) Any Freemasonry content would enrich the experience of theosophists who were involved in the Egyptian Freemasonry, under the leadership of Rudolf Steiner, when they contemplated this painting. Also, for those theosophists, and later anthroposophists, who were not in the Masonic groups, and never would be, the painting with these Masonic elements would also enrich their experience of its message, because these powerfully evocative elements can speak powerfully to the soul, without any presence of Masonic knowledge.

Seated on a throne is king Solomon, in a pale blue colour. Opposite him, in a reddish colour, standing upright, is Hiram, the master builder whom king Solomon invited to work on his famous temple, to bring it to completion. Standing between these two men, is Balkis, the Queen of Sheba, who is enveloped in a kind of swirling blue aura, which spreads out far around her, see illustration 5. Over-arching these three people, is a sequence of zodiac symbols. Before we begin to contemplate this scene, we need to note that King Solomon is shown here holding a pastoral crook, even though, since he was a king, one would think that he would hold a regal object. The reason for this is that, when the painting was carefully examined under magnification, the faded outline of a pastoral staff is quite evident. But, in contrast, the head-dress of Solomon has remained unclear. The figure of Hiram and the queen of Sheba are reasonably clear.

### King Solomon and Hiram Abiff

The narrative about these two men, in the First Book of Kings, (Chapter 6), has become a major theme in Freemasonry. Rudolf Steiner had been leading a small number of his students, who were Theosophists with Masonic interests, in carrying out Masonic rituals, for about eight years prior to the creating of this painting. Consequently he gave these people some lectures on the general theme of king Solomon's temple, which can help us understand this scene. These rituals were of a kind that were regarded by the mainstream Masonic movement as non-authoritative or 'heretical' texts, quite outside the 'proper' Masonic movement.

In regard to Solomon, Rudolf Steiner revealed that pre-Golgotha initiates were very closely linked to their ethnic group or nation. In their initiation experience they received the guiding principles or 'laws' from the spiritual realms which were to govern their folk; and in this secret initiatory rite, they saw into the spiritual worlds. But such initiates had to a make a sacrifice; they were linked to the sins committed by their people against these laws or governing principles. King Solomon belonged to this type of initiate, and such an initiate had to constantly re-incarnate in his own folk. But there were others in antiquity who were not initiates, but who were nevertheless gifted and intelligent souls, and were drawing near to being initiated. These souls were often solitary people, separate from any specific folk, and gathered their insights primarily

---

[15] GA 265, p. 416.

from their experiences of this world, and in this way gradually attained to wisdom.[16] Hiram was such a person; he could apply his wisdom practically to life. In this case Hiram applied his expertise to co-operating in the building of King Solomon's temple, which is as we shall see, a great spiritual task, and not a physical temple. (Although a physical temple was also built; just not to the designs given in the Bible.) Hiram is described as 'the son of a widow' in one of the two accounts about him in the Bible (1Kings: 5). As Rudolf Steiner explained, this phrase amongst initiated people in antiquity was a veiled way of saying that the person was actively involved in the spiritual path. They used this expression, because they felt that, in contrast to humanity in earlier millennia, guidance from the divine beings in spirit realms was now gone. This inner guidance was called "the Father". So the soul was now a widow, and the ego or self was "the son" of this soul who was no longer guided, so the people seeking initiation were in effect trying to re-establish a connection to their higher self.[17]

In the Freemason movement, probably in the 18th century, the word 'Abiff' was added to his name.[18] The actual origin and meaning of this term is unclear in this context; it is twice used of Hiram in 2Chronicles (4:11). This Hebrew word can mean 'father', but it can also mean something like 'master craftsman'. The unknown Freemason who added this term as an epithet to Hiram obviously was pointing to this second meaning: Hiram 'the master craftsman'. We should note that the head-scarf of Hiram appears in the original glass plate as bluish, yet only in the upper part of it, for the lower section is white. This unusual colouring scheme is still to be seen in the painting shown here, but it is possible that the bluish tinge on the upper part is due to degradation of the old colour photograph, and not intended.

**King Solomon's Temple**
Now the question arises, why are these two men depicted here? They figure largely in Freemasonry, because the building of Solomon's temple serves as an allegory for spiritual development. That these two men are involved in the task of building a spiritual temple, rather than a physical one, is indicated by Rudolf Steiner when he implies that in fact, the magnificent, lavish and esoterically designed temple was never actually built. In one lecture, he stated, *"Has anyone ever seen it? Herodotus journeyed right through Palestine in 500 BC and did not mention it."*[19]

It becomes clear that the Biblical description of the temple is more referring to qualities of the soul and spirit; see illustration 6 for a simplified diagrammatic outline of the temple. Nevertheless, Solomon did indeed build a physical temple, but not of the design detailed in the Bible. During his reign a normal temple was built; this occurred about 1,000 BC. It was later attacked by the Egyptian Pharaoh, Sehshonq, or Shishak, in about the year 924 BC. Later, the Israelites, led by Jehoash partially rebuilt it, about 835 BC.

It is unknown when the Masonic movement took up the theme of king Solomon's temple as descriptive of esoteric initiatory themes. The earliest document concerning the medieval craft of masonry as such, (not yet the actual 'speculative' or esoteric Freemasonry movement within Europe) dates from AD 1254. There is no reference to Solomon's temple in this document.[20] But historians are aware that long before the Freemasons became a known movement, the spiritual significance of Solomon's temple was noted and commented on by great Biblical scholars already back in the 8th century, such as the Venerable Bede in England, and Alcuin in the Frankish empire of Charlemagne. Bede stated that, "it was designed in the shape of the Universal Church". An image of this temple was also placed in an Irish cathedral, but it was stolen in AD 1129. Likewise an image of the temple was depicted in Amiens Cathedral in about AD 1230. So what is the deep secret of this temple, that has caused it to exert so potent an influence in Christendom?

---

[16] GA 265, p. 406.
[17] GA 93 *The Temple Legend*, lecture, 11th Nov. 1904, p.72.
[18] The first Freemason manuscript to mention Abiff is the *Inigo Jones Ms.,* dated 1607, but probably written about 1725.
[19] GA 286 p. 24.
[20] The earliest Masonic document to mention this temple is dated AD 1410, but curiously, it discretely draws on much earlier information, written or oral, which is of unknown antiquity.

## 6 King Solomon's Temple

**Above**: the side view, with the curtain before the Holy of Holies (purple).
**Below**: the floor-plan, with the stairs before the Holy of Holies, where Solomon, the Queen of Sheba, Hiram are standing, in the painting.

Rudolf Steiner reveals the profound secret of the symbolism of this temple; the complex Biblical description of Solomon's temple is alluding to two esoteric themes. One is an architectural presentation of the path of the neophyte who seeks to develop the Spirit-self, as Rudolf Steiner commented when referring to Solomon's temple, "***The temple: that is the human being who receives into his soul, the Spirit***".[21] Such spiritual development effort also has an impact on the Earth itself,

> The Freemason is above striving to advance to the point that he may be a worthy co-worker at the building of humanity and the world. The purpose of earthly existence is that we re-shape our world as it goes through its evolutionary periods. Human activity makes ever more impact upon the Earth. What shall the Earth become? A building which the human being completes. And it is the duty of every person to work at this building. In this {symbolic} temple-complex, three columns must be incorporated, or otherwise, chaos shall result. The columns on which this temple shall rest are: wisdom, beauty and strength.[22]

The other meaning of King Solomon's temple is extraordinary; it has to do with the actual structure of the future, more spiritualized, body of the human being. The body's structure has to be envisaged, as an Idea (or astral-Devachanic image) in advance, if humanity is to achieve this goal in the future. Rudolf Steiner explained this,

> If we could have an overview of millennia not only centuries, then we would see that even the human body's form is oriented towards the thoughts, feelings and mental images formed over millennia. And the great guiding Powers in the evolving of humanity give to people, in right time-frame, the correct mental images, so that the human body itself can {in the future} be transformed... From whence comes the present-day length and breadth and width of the human body? It is the outcome of that which was formerly in the astral body and etheric body. There were present already: thoughts, mental images and feelings.

He then proceeds to tell his audience that they can more easily understand this theme if they consider a fact already known to them about life after death,; how the soul newly released from the body, feels as if it is widening out, to a huge extent, becoming expanded on a large scale, out into all directions, because of how the etheric body expands. He then goes on to say,

> This seeing of the etheric body, expanded out in very large dimensions, is a very important mental image that the human being has; for in the Atlantean Age this very mental image had to be awakened, as the etheric body was not then in such a close connection with the physical body as it later was with people in the post-Atlantean Age. Thus this mental image had first to be awakened. If a person pictures to themselves approximately that greatly expanded size, which people today experience when they become larger (in their etheric} after death, then that person has now formed the cause, the {causative} thought-form, which was needed {long ago} to bring the physical body into {what would become} its current dimensions.

> That is to say, when the person at the time when the etheric body is separated from the physical body, has the correct dimensions of the {future} physical body presented to them {as a thought-form} then these dimensions **form themselves into the shape which the body has today**. And these forms were brought about mainly by the leaders of humanity's evolution. In the various stories of the Great Flood, exact details are to be found {regarding the dimensions of the physical body of post-Atlantean people.} If you think of the human being circumscribed with approximately the forms which the etheric body must have, in order that the physical body of the human being forms itself in the right way, then you have the proportions of Noah's Ark.

---

[21] GA 286, 12th Dec. 1911.
[22] GA 265, p. 234

Rudolf Steiner then proceeds to explain that the proportions of the Ark – 50 x 30 x 300 – correspond to those of the human body's width, depth and height. He then proceeds to refer to the temple of king Solomon,

> Humanity then went from the Atlantean epoch over into the Post-Atlantean epoch. In the next large epoch {which starts around AD 8000}, the human body shall again be of a different type; and so humanity in this epoch now needs to experience those thought-forms which are able to provide the causative factors which shall result in the body, in that future epoch, having the correct dimensions... ...these thought-forms are in the dimensions specified for king Solomon's temple. The dimensions of this temple represent, once they are realised in the physical body, in a deeply symbolic way, the over-all structure of the physical body of humanity in the sixth Large Epoch.[23]

The work of forming the archetypal Idea of future humanity's physical form is an exalted work of initiates. In our painting, the two men allude to these two esoteric processes, both of which are deeply connected to what the Queen of Sheba represents.

**The Queen of Sheba with King Solomon and Hiram**
Masonic themes, symbols and artwork, derive from a devout and esoteric inspiration, although it is especially through Rudolf Steiner that their significance can be discovered. The meeting of the Queen of Sheba with King Solomon does not generally play a role in Masonic rituals, but every year each Masonic lodge holds an 'installation' ceremony, in which a new Worshipful Master takes up his role and also appoints fellow officers for that year. As this ceremony commences, the passage in the Bible, about the meeting of Queen of Sheba with King Solomon is read out (1 Kings: 10). This passage relates how this foreign ruler came with a huge amount of precious goods, including gold, as a gift to the king. The passage tells us that she wanted to meet him in order ascertain just how wise he was, and to do this, she plied him with riddles. This narrative is concealing the process of someone seeking esoteric wisdom, who wants to find out how initiated the king is, and to what extent she could enter into such esoteric wisdom. It is understood that this event, historically, involved a queen of the Sabaeans of Arabia, some 1,400 miles away; a journey that would have taken six months, each way. (Ethiopian and Arabic texts add much detail to the Biblical narrative.)

The Masonic ceremony tells us that the Queen came in order to see for herself the magnificent (symbolic) temple, and that she entered into his magnificent temple in a highly colourful, elaborate ceremony. The Masonic legends relates how the Queen was personally attracted first to King Solomon, whom she marries, but she later became attracted to Hiram. The Bible does not mention a wedding or any of these complex relationships. The Ethiopian Christians believe that there was such a wedding and that they themselves are the descendants of the son born to the Queen, from king Solomon. The figure of the Queen of Sheba, whilst not directly prominent in Freemason rituals, has a subtle presence. For example, during one ritual, a devout text is recited and those present throw up their hands and also roll their eyes upwards, as a sign of devotion – for this is understood to be what the Queen of Sheba did, upon experiencing the wisdom of Solomon.

This high position of a woman in Freemasonry is a significant paradox, when one factors in the centuries-old exclusion of women from membership in Masonry, until the 20th century (except sporadically in some minor, separate rituals as from the 18th century). We need to note too here, that Masonic historians report that some lodges have removed this reference to Queen of Sheba in the installation ceremony.[24] But where the various references to the Queen are to be found, this paradox points to the role of the Queen of Sheba as being symbolic. It is reported that an impressive painting is placed on a wall in many Masonic Lodges, depicting the meeting of the Queen of Sheba with King Solomon. Called, *The Meeting of Solomon and the Queen of Sheba*, it is painted by Edward A. Poynter (1836-1919); see illustration 7.

---

[23] GA 101, lecture 28th Dec. 1907.
[24] *The Etiquette of Freemasonry: A Handbook for the Brethren,* An Old Past Master, Skyhorse publishing, 2012.

7  *The Queen of Sheba meets King Solomon,* by E. A. Poynter

In the Anna May picture, it is the dynamic between the Queen of Sheba and the two men which is the main focus underlying the pivotal theme of building Solomon's temple. Rudolf Steiner refers to her as 'Balkis', a name of Arabic origin: a name which is used for her in Freemasonry. We have noted that one esoteric process which the Temple symbolizes concerns the pathway that the spiritually striving soul has to journey along towards enlightenment or spirituality. In our painting the Queen with her symbolic head-dress, as with other feminine figures in mystical literature, symbolizes this soul seeking to attain higher consciousness. But this attainment can be achieved by one of two pathways. By either passively receiving cosmic inspiration through the chaste, withdrawn meditative path or by engaging powerfully in earthly activity and through trial and error, and the exercise of initiative, learning to refine and to more insightfully direct one's will.

These two different pathways to wisdom and spirituality are represented by Solomon and Hiram, respectively. So on this esoteric level, this section of the painting depicts the spiritualizing soul – the Queen of Sheba – deciding between the pure, non-earthly cosmic wisdom represented by king Solomon, and the wisdom that is achieved by conquering the lower earthly self, through intensive earthly activity, represented by Hiram. Therefore Solomon is painted in a delicate blue, alluding to auric colour of the meditative, prayerful soul and perhaps also the blue firmament above, which acts as a kind of doorway to the cosmos.

### The High Priest's breastplate

On Solomon's chest is the famous Breastplate, which is a thick piece of cloth, to which a series of twelve semi-precious stones were attached by gold wire. These twelve gemstones are obviously representing the zodiac, showing again that Solomon is linked to the cosmos. In this way, although he is a king, he holds a shepherd's crook, for here he is representing wisdom, which in response to his tranquil and pure qualities, is passively received, relatively speaking, from the cosmos. (The pastoral crook is still faintly visible on the 1912 glass-plate colour photograph, and on the 1975 poster, under magnification.) This breastplate tells us that Solomon communes with spiritual forces operative from the zodiac. The cosmic power of this zodiacal arrangement, which was referred to as a kind of oracle in the Bible, is testified to by the famous historian Josephus, who writes that,

> ...so great a splendour shone forth from them {the 12 jewels} before the army began to march, that all people were aware of God being present, to help them...but this breastplate stopped being radiant two hundred years before I wrote this book...[25]

Josephus was writing about AD 93-94. In this 'breastplate' made of strong woven cloth, there were also small pockets in which the mysterious Urim and Thummin were kept. These two objects are mentioned in the Bible as the means by which the high priests of the Hebrews received inspiration as to the will of their god.

These two men here, as in Freemasonry generally, represent the esoteric significance subtly placed in the Bible text about the two sons of Adam: Cain and Abel. Solomon represents the Abel type of human being. Abel does not invent tools, nor apply any basic engineering capacity in his work; he simply receives what the fertility of the Earth gives to him as animals and plants. This occurs naturally through the interaction of the Earth and the cosmos. In contrast to Solomon, Hiram is dressed in a reddish garment, alluding to the red blood that carries the earthly desires and ego. Hiram holds a metal tool and is standing upright, one foot forwards, ready for activity. He represents the Cain type of human being, which means the type of soul who seeks wisdom through being involved in earthly goals and projects. Hence he is impelled to develop and use tools made of wood or metals to transform earthly matter.

We saw earlier, that Solomon's Temple represents the structure and dynamics of the human soul as it moves towards the spirit. But the powerful, evocative image here also has another significance, which is unveiled when the second meaning of Solomon's Temple is contemplated.

---

[25] Josephus, *The Antiquities of the Jews*, Book 3: 217-218.

We noted above that this second meaning concerns the profoundly esoteric task of forming an Idea of the future, more spiritualized, human being. The detailed description of Solomon's temple given in the Bible, had to do with this pivotal, archetypal thought-form, which manifests the correct structure and dimensions of the form that the human being must have in the next large cultural Epoch, as the Spirit-self emerges.[26]

In the anthroposophical view of the future, this next large Epoch is the 6th large Epoch, which we can call the Manichaean Epoch; it shall commence about AD 8000, after the War of All against All. Those who contemplate the description of king Solomon's temple in Scripture, or work with it in terms of Masonic rituals and lessons, are being assisted to sense this archetypal image of the future human being. The sacred esoteric depths of Scripture are revealed by these words of Rudolf Steiner. A very important insight as to the mystery of the idea of Solomon's Temple as embodying the structure of the human spirit derived from the cosmos, is revealed in the writings of the Jewish esotericist, Philo of Alexandria (first century AD). He wrote in regard to the veil inside the temple, which curtained off the doors which led into the sanctuary called the Holy of Holies that, "the veil was woven {contained images} of just so many things as the world is made of, for it {symbolises} the universal Temple, which existed before the holy {historical} temple".[27] So on the second level, this section of the great painting is depicting the initiate Solomon – helped by Hiram, who is nearing initiation – contemplating the future spiritual reality of humanity. These two are creating the Idea or thought-form of the human being in the future, especially those human beings who are seeking to develop the Spirit-self (which is also called the Spiritual-self). To complete our consideration of this scene, we need to contemplate further features in the image of the Queen of Sheba.

**The Queen of Sheba & the Spirit-self**
We see a feminine figure, within a kind of aura that sweeps out around her, and which is a radiant blue colour; just as with Solomon, this colour suggests cosmic wisdom. There are several special features about her. Firstly, she has an unusual head-dress. Secondly, she is holding a green stone. Thirdly, there are some fine lines unobtrusively connecting her head-dress to an astrological feature. So what is this figure telling us? Firstly, with regard to her head-dress, I have attempted to clarify the details here, although it was not possible to make clear all of the geometrical forms in this. As we saw in illustration 5, it appears to be a stylized lotus flower, with a jewel in it. The lotus is flowering above the stylized surface of a water pond, which is also suggestive of a lunar crescent. We have noted above that the Queen of Sheba represents the soul on the path to spirituality. She is called by Rudolf Steiner,

> the deeply perceiving person, someone who recognizes actual wisdom.[28]

The green stone she is holding depicts the Holy Grail, as described in a some versions of the Holy Grail legends. The Holy Grail is defined in medieval Grail literature, and by Rudolf Steiner, in a variety of ways. Here it is the gemstone which, as the Grail legend from Wolfram von Eschenbach declares, fell from the crown of Lucifer, when Lucifer was cast out of heaven. This story is indicating that the Spiritual-self is attained as a result of overcoming the lower astral qualities instilled into the astral body through the influence of Lucifer. But as anthroposophy teaches, it is necessary to have an earthly ego with its lower desires in the first stage, in order to eventually achieve a higher ego. It was the outcome of Lucifer's influence which resulted in humanity developing a sense of self, or an earthly ego.

The extensive heavenly-blue auric field indicates the presence of cosmic wisdom living in this soul. The cosmic wisdom is indicated by the delicate blue glow, encompassing the zodiac energies, which spreads out above her head; this interaction is shown in the form of faint rays of spiritual energy between her head and the bluish cosmic glow. As Rudolf Steiner explained, in the person who is developing the spiritual-soul, and taking this intuitive consciousness further,

---

[26] GA 101, lecture, 28th Dec. 1907.
[27] The Writings of Philo, *Questions and Answers on Exodus*, 2:85.
[28] GA 93, p. 171.

towards the actual Spiritual-self, his or her higher soul forces unite with the incoming cosmic reality.[29] The interweaving of the Spirit-self here with the zodiac is also an indicator of the relationship of our Spirit-human (or Atma) – the highest aspect of the human spirit – to the zodiac. This part of our spiritual potential is developed when the cosmic will that has brought forth our physical body, and exists subconsciously as a will-force within us, is accessed by the spiritualized soul, consciously. As Rudolf Steiner taught, the physical body becomes transformed by the initiate into the Spirit-human.

### Hail to the jewel in the lotus !
That the Queen of Sheba is holding the Grail stone suggests that she is consciously seeking to transform Lucifer's influence. In addition to these features, it is her head-dress that tells us another message of this scene. The image of 'a jewel in the lotus' is directly referring to the famous ancient Indian mantra, "Aum mani padme hum", which means "Hail to the jewel in the lotus, amen". As I wrote in *The Way to the Sacred*,

> The 'jewel in the lotus-flower' refers to the presence of the divine eternal-self which becomes present in the astral body as it flowers; that is, as the chakras form. However this eternal-self, as it manifests gradually in human evolution, shall transform the physical body, into the clear, radiant 'soft-diamond' body, in the far future. Hence the higher-self will have this jewel-like presence in the current initiate, or in future humankind.

So, this famous and profound sentence has some substantial nuances in it. It is in effect a respectful greeting to the primeval self; and it is defining this as an incorruptible spiritual jewel of light which exists in the soul. It is also implying that this is one's higher-self of the future. The lotus flower meant here is very likely the white lotus flower; it is the only aquatic plant that flowers with its seeds fully formed. So the essence of its life-forces (the seeds) and its blossom are present at the same time. Its blossom is the result of its 'soul quality' permeating its reproductive capacity with beauty. This combination serves as a very fine symbol of the Spiritual-self, which is beginning to experience the developing of the Life-Spirit. The lotus grows in water, and water is a well-known symbol of the astral body. The white lotus blossoms in the night-time. Hence the suggestion, underneath the flower, of both water and a crescent moon; the moon is of course a symbol of the night. The night blossoming is similar to the flowers blossoming like stars, in a night sky, in a profound Rosicrucian image, the *Mons Philosophorum or Mountain of the Sage*; see illustration 8. In this esoteric artwork, the tree which is blossoming, is on the night side of the mountain. The development of the spiritual-self takes place on a level which is obscured from the normal awareness of the meditating person, so it occurs, so to speak, in the night.

### The Veil before the Holy of Holies
Behind the feminine figure of the Queen of Sheba, or our own Spiritual-self, there is a pale blue, curtain-like background. This feature brings the scene into the temple of Solomon, for this curtain-like background represents the veil or curtain which covered the entrance to the Holy of Holies in Solomon's Temple. A careful look at the bluish veil behind the Queen of Sheba will show a number of faintly visible faces, but unfortunately I could not make these any clearer. This feature of the painting is very significant, when we know the instructions for the veil or curtain which was to be inside the original portable tabernacle, before the Hebrews could settle permanently in the Holy Lands. The Book of Exodus states, "Moreover you shall make the tabernacle with curtains of fine woven linen, and blue, purple and scarlet thread; with artistic designs of cherubs, you shall weave them." (Exod.26:1-6)

This arrangement was copied centuries later when Solomon built a permanent temple. In the actual temple, as re-built and repaired in Jerusalem over the centuries, and thus known historically, some of the features of the ideal Solomon's temple were replicated. Reports about the temple that existed in the Hellenistic era do still exist. In regard to the veil before the Holy of

---

[29] For example, in GA 55, lecture of 28th March 1907.

Holies, we learn from Josephus, the historian, (first century AD) that to him and presumably to others, the colour scheme embodied in this veil was fourfold and hence alluded to the 'elements'; these would have represented the four ethers. Josephus also recounts that the zodiac was represented,

> ....before these doors there was a veil of equal largeness with the doors. It was a Babylonian curtain, embroidered with blue, and fine linen, and scarlet, and purple, and of a texture that was truly wonderful. Nor was this mixture of colours without its mystical interpretation, but was a kind of image of the universe; for by the scarlet there seemed to be enigmatically signified fire, by the fine flax the earth, by the blue the air, and by the purple the sea; two of them having their colours the foundation of this resemblance; but the fine flax and the purple have their own origin for that foundation, the earth producing the one, and the sea the other. This curtain had also embroidered upon it all that was mystical in the heavens, excepting that of the [twelve] signs, representing living creatures.[30]

So in the painting, this scene is a contemplation (or astral 'imagination') about the spiritually striving soul, as placed between the Abel and the Cain pathways to the spirit. A vital part of this contemplation is that king Solomon, Queen Balkis and Master craftsman Hiram are actually meeting deep inside Solomon's Temple, very near to the veil hanging before the entrance to the Holy of Holies; see illustration 6. How near are they? According to Scripture (Isaiah 6:1), there were some stairs leading up to the entrance to the Holy of Holies (called the *Debir* in Hebrew), because its floor was higher than the floor of the main section of the temple (called the *Hekhal* in Hebrew). As you can see, these three people or symbolic figures being at the top of the stairs are in fact located right outside the actual entrance into the Holy of Holies. Solomon, as an initiate, is somewhat nearer than Hiram, who is a few steps further down.

So far, we have seen that the Queen of Sheba represents our soul as it begins the task of developing itself spiritually, and that it is by transforming the forces from Lucifer that this step is to be achieved. Also we have seen that the influence of the Grail shall be guiding and leading this process; and this means influences from the Christ-impulse. We shall explore the Grail mysteries further when we consider the middle section of the painting. So, specifically, the Queen of Sheba represents the development of the Spiritual-self out of the soul or astral body, with the potential for the Life-Spirit to begin to arise. In addition to these truths, in this section of the painting there is a fascinating indicator as to the zodiacal Ages involved here.

**The Zodiac Ages involved here**
There is a very important veiled message about the zodiacal timing of the scene we have been exploring. For above the three people here, there is a sequence of traditional zodiac symbols, but it is not the usual sequence, see illustration 5. At the far right of this sequence, above and a little behind Hiram, we can see the symbol for Aries, and next to this, towards the left, is Pisces. Whereas on the far left of this scene, behind Solomon, is the symbol for Gemini, and further behind him there was presumably the symbol for Taurus, although this symbol can not be seen in the painting, even when examined under magnification. The absence of the symbol here for Taurus suggests that the normal sequence is incomplete. For this absence to be deliberate would be extremely unusual, so there are two possible explanations. Firstly, the area where one would expect the symbol for Taurus to be drawn, is quite dark, so possibly the 1912 photograph may not have been able to record it; a careful inspection of that general location under magnification does show an unclear patch, as if something may have been drawn there.

So one possibility is that Rudolf Steiner did intend for the Taurus symbol to be painted here. That would of course clearly spell out that this zodiac starts with Taurus – and that tells the viewer that the scene involving King Solomon, the Queen of Sheba and Hiram is to be dated to the Age of Taurus. The second possibility is that Rudolf Steiner specifically left the symbol for Taurus out of the picture. Such an incomplete zodiac is very strange, but the message embedded

---

[30] From Josephus, *Wars* 5.5.4.

**8 Mons Philosophorum:** three stars are growing in the night-side of the mountain.
(the shadow-night side, indicated originally only by shadow, has been accentuated by me, AA)

in that would be the same as having the Taurus symbol placed there at the beginning of the sequence: namely, that this zodiac sequence starts with Taurus. That is, since Taurus has to be somewhere in every zodiac, here it has to be near to Solomon, because its place is always next to Gemini. So, the scene with king Solomon then refers to Taurus, instead of a symbol.

In any case, the sequence of zodiac signs here is unusual, because the zodiac of course usually starts with Aries and ends in Pisces. But here it starts (on the left) with Gemini, (or with Taurus in some subtle way), and ends in Aries, over on the right side. I have concluded that the symbol for Taurus was actually painted there originally, and has faded off. What we can say is, that the Age in which the work of creating Solomon's temple was undertaken, was the Taurean Age, which started in 2907 BC and ended in 747 BC. Historically king Solomon and Hiram lived in that Age, approximately between the years 1050 BC to 950 BC.

This unusual zodiacal sequence also has the advantage that the Age of Pisces is far in the future; because here the symbol for Pisces is located over to the right side, near to the large column. Now we need to note that there are in fact two faint lines running from the head-ornament of the Queen of Sheba across to the symbol for Pisces. More precisely, these two lines meet at an intriguing feature just underneath the Pisces symbol; this feature resembles an armillary sphere to some extent, see illustration 9. An armillary sphere or astrolabe is a spherical framework made of metal rings which depict the Earth in space, in relation to celestial bodies. So the astrolabe shows the ecliptic and the equinoctial points, (these are to do with the path of the sun around the earth) and the equator. These spheres could also show the longitudes and latitudes, depending on the purpose of the device.

An object of this kind points our attention towards space, towards the solar system. But actually, here the three-dimensional sphere, made up of dotted lines, appears to be an unusual depiction of the Earth, rather than a proper armillary sphere. Now, if in our mind, we combine these two – the Earth and an armillary sphere, with its focus on the solar system – we are directed to the zodiacal Ages, marking out the sequence of zodiacal Ages on the Earth, caused by the relative motion of the Earth and the sun. For these Ages are determined by the motion of the sun in space, through the zodiac, as experienced from the Earth.

Now, the two faint lines going from the Queen of Sheba over to Pisces, which has this unusual sphere below it, is indicating that, it will be in the Age of Pisces, long after the Age of Taurus, when human beings may begin developing their higher self. This starts with the spiritual-soul or intuitive, insightful consciousness, and leads eventually to the Spiritual-self, the 'jewel in the lotus'. And for us of course, that time is now, for the Age of Pisces commenced in AD 1413, and continues until AD 3573.

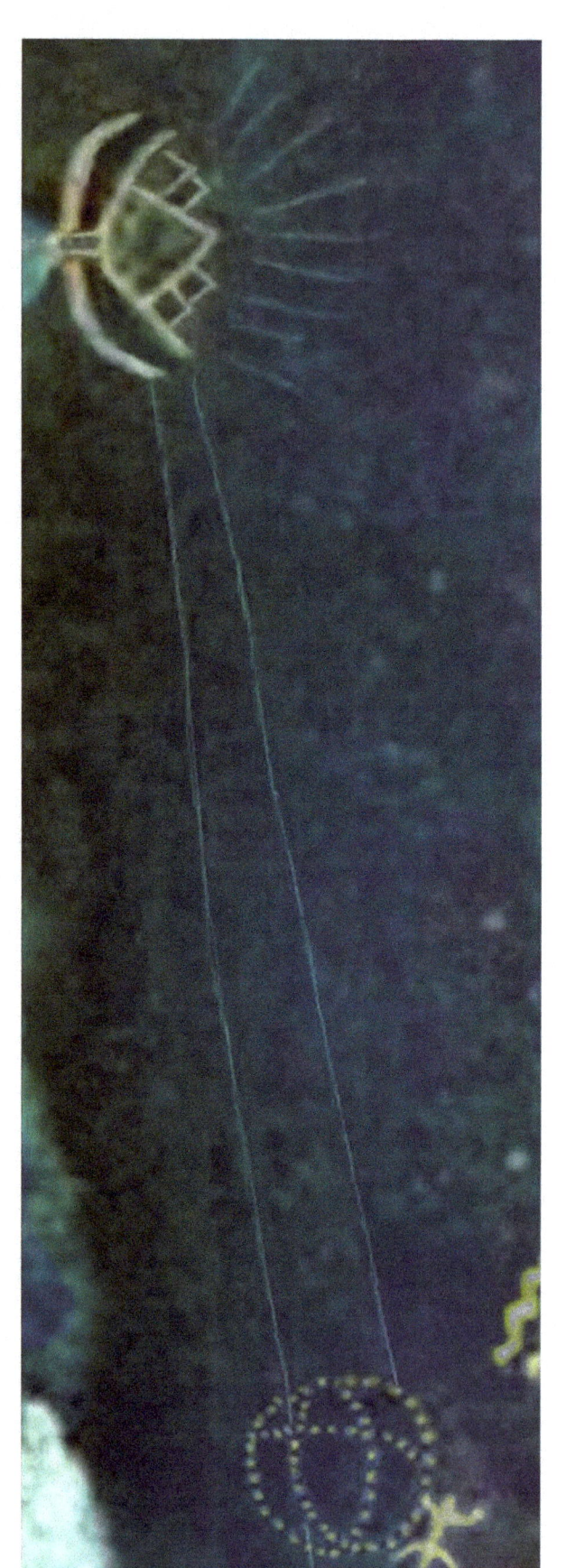

9  **Two lines from the Queen to the Armillry Sphere, indicating the Piscean Age**
(These two faint lines are visible under magnification, here they have been slightly enhanced.)

# The Left Side, below

## Moses, the burning bush and the Menorah

Directly underneath the stairs in the temple leading to the Holy of Holies, is a remarkable scene. To the right, kneeling down, is Moses, see illustration 10. He is facing the burning bush, the flaming branches of which have been metamorphosed here into a menorah or candle-stick holder; the branches of the bush have become seven burning candles. This feature of our painting is of course directly referring to the event, reported in the Book of Exodus, (chapt. 3) wherein Moses sees a bush which appears to be burning. However, the bush is not actually burning, rather it is a spiritual (clairvoyant) experience that Moses is having. This is how it is translated in the NIV,

> [Ex 3:1] Now Moses was tending the flock of Jethro his father-in-law, the priest of Midian, and he led the flock to the far side of the desert and came to Horeb, the mountain of God. [Ex 3:2] There the angel of the LORD appeared to him in flames of fire from within a bush. Moses saw that though the bush was on fire it did not burn up.
> [Ex 3:3] So Moses thought, "I will go over and see this strange sight -- why the bush does not burn up." [Ex 3:4] When the LORD saw that he had gone over to look, God called to him from within the bush, "Moses! Moses !" And Moses said, "Here I am."
> [Ex 3:5] "Do not come any closer," God said. "Take off your sandals, for the place where you are standing is holy ground." [Ex 3:6] Then he said, "I am the God of your father, the God of Abraham, the God of Isaac and the God of Jacob." At this, Moses hid his face, because he was afraid to look at God. [Ex 3:7] The LORD said, "I have indeed seen the misery of my people in Egypt. I have heard them crying out because of their slave drivers, and I am concerned about their suffering.
>
> [Ex 3:8] So I have come down to rescue them from the hand of the Egyptians and to bring them up out of that land into a good and spacious land, a land flowing with milk and honey[g] – the home of the Canaanites, Hittites, Amorites, Perizzites, Hivites and Jebusites. [Ex 3:9] And now the cry of the Israelites has reached me, and I have seen the way the Egyptians are oppressing them.
> [Ex 3:10] So now, go. I am sending you to Pharaoh to bring my people the Israelites out of Egypt." [Ex 3:11] But Moses said to God, "Who am I, that I should go to Pharaoh and bring the Israelites out of Egypt?"
> [Ex 3:12] And God said, "I will be with you. And this will be the sign to you that it is I who have sent you: When you have brought the people out of Egypt, you will worship God on this mountain "
>
> [Ex 3:13] **Moses said to God, "Suppose I go to the Israelites and say to them, 'The God of your fathers has sent me to you,' and they ask me, 'What is his name?' Then what shall I tell them?"**
> [Ex 3:14] **God said to Moses, "I AM WHO I AM. This is what you are to say to the Israelites: 'I AM has sent me to you.' "**

It is the words that I have put into bold fonts that we need to contemplate, to understand the painting. Here Moses is experiencing the awe-inspiring moment, when from this bush, the great divine being speaks to Moses about what Divine Will has set him apart to do. Moses is about to be given his mission which requires him to return to Egypt, and to then persuade the Pharaoh to let the Hebrew tribes-people emigrate so that they may eventually settle in the Holy Lands, and establish the nation of Israel. So Moses asks the Divine Being what is His name, so that he may an authority amongst his fellow Hebrews, when he announces that "God" wants the exodus of the Hebrews from Egypt to happen.

## Understanding the "I am the I am"

So Moses asks, what shall I tell my people is the name of the God who has sent me to them? The deity answers, giving his name in a phrase, which has never been clearly explained; the phrase is normally translated as *"I am that I am"*, or *"I am who I am"*. It is this moment which Moses is

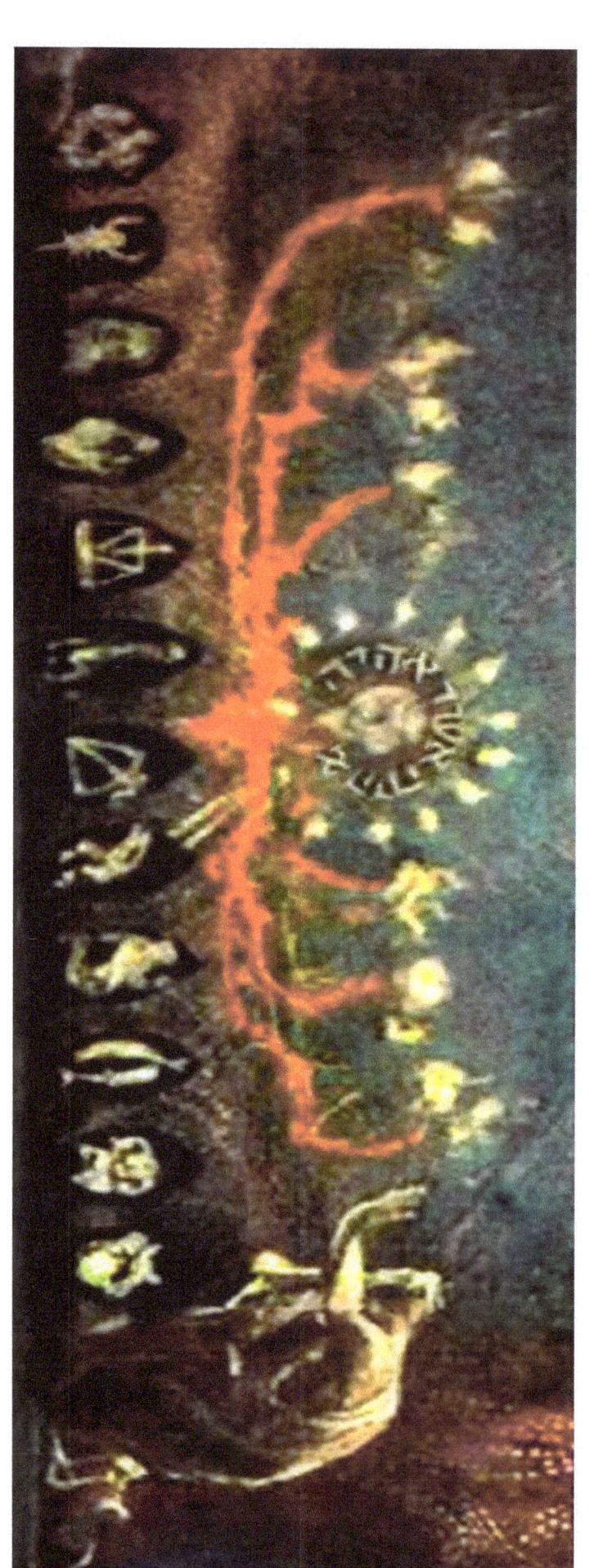

**10 Moses hears God from the menorah-burning-bush**
Note below is the zodiac and two lines of energy proceed from the bush to Capricorn

experiencing here in the painting. But this 'name' is a complex and baffling Hebrew phrase, which thus remains a sacred mystery. This is because the Hebrew phrase, 'ehyeh asher ehyeh', (ín Hebrew: אֶהְיֶה אֲשֶׁר אֶהְיֶה), contains part of the verb 'to be' in a way which can refer to the past, or to the present, or to the future. A reader can only know to which of these three tenses it refers by seeing the context of the sentence; that is the nature of the ancient Hebrew language. Here, there is almost no context, (except that "I was" is ruled out, because the Divine Being obviously exists.) So what does this remarkable answer to Moses actually mean? The first part of it could be either, *I was* or, *I am*, or *I will be*. So translators are baffled, and usually decide either on, "I **am** that (or who) I **am**" or "I **will be** that (or who) I **will be**".

Whether it means the present or the future is unclear. So lofty, unusual and baffling is this statement that some primary Jewish religious texts, referring to this in another language such as Aramaic, leave the phrase untranslated. Rudolf Steiner wishes to demonstrate that it is implicit in the words to Moses that the eternal, divine self within the human being is itself from God. In other words, that 'God' (Jahve-Christ) *is* the divine true ego within the human being. So, Rudolf Steiner does not translate the phrase where God names himself as: "I was, am, will be *that* I was, am, will be". He does not involve that eternal quality of "was, am and will be", instead, he lets that stay in the background and takes up the simplified version, of "I am *that* I am", but he changes it in a remarkable way. He translates it as saying: "I am *the* I am". He tells his audiences that the phrase is saying that God is the (innermost core) of the human being's sense of self, the "I":

> I [God] **am** *the* **I am** [of human beings].

But in fact, such an understanding of this phrase does not seem to have ever occurred to scholars of the Judaic-Christian religions; and it would be rejected as incorrect to the grammar. The major reason that they have not viewed the phrase in Rudolf Steiner's way, is no doubt the fact that the word normally translated as "that" or "who" (asher, אֲשֶׁר) is never translated as "**the**" ("I am *the* I am"). Scholars would say that such a translation is an error. But in fact this word 'asher' can be understood to mean "the" or "of the". So Rudolf Steiner's translation is not an error; see Appendix Two for a more detailed assessment of this passage from the Hebrew.

So in Rudolf Steiner's version, the phrase takes on an extraordinary, sacred meaning. Namely, that the higher ego of the human being *is* God, or, derives from God. The term 'God', which in non-esoteric cultural usage is somewhat abstract, here means an interweaving of two of the seven Powers or 'Elohim', namely Yahweh and the cosmic Christ (but it is not limited to even these). This is a deeply potent spiritual statement.

So, if we allow the second occurrence of the term "I am" to refer to the human being's own sense of self, and not to God, as Rudolf Steiner teaches, then the words from the burning bush imply that God is inherently bound inwardly to the human being's "I". But this extraordinary revelation, being made at the onset of a migration of people out of Egypt, who were to pioneer a religion which would assist the development of an individualized ego-sense, is still not fully clear. For real clarity, we need to include in our contemplations, the adjacent features of the painting: the Menorah bush and the zodiac.


**The two horns of Moses**
Before we explore the further nuances of this part of the painting we need to also note that there is a slightly strange contour in the way the head of Moses is drawn. This is intended to discreetly draw attention to the fact that, according to an old Biblical tradition, Moses had two horns. That Rudolf Steiner has arranged for this feature to be included, validates this tradition. This description has its origin in the original Hebrew words used to describe the appearance of Moses as he came down from the mountain, after meeting God and receiving the Ten Commandments. The Hebrew expression here is ambiguous and hence quite obscure, a situation which is often a sign that an esoteric truth is being discreetly communicated. St. Jerome, when translating the

Hebrew account of Moses into Latin, decided to say, (when his Latin is put into English) "his face was horned from the conversation with the Lord." (Exod. 34:29,35) Since the vowels were not written down originally in the old Hebrew text, a word in this phrase could be understood as either the Hebrew word 'qaran' (to have horns) or 'qeren' (to shine). Writers on this topic have often incorrectly stated that Jerome misunderstood the Hebrew, but this is not the case. He was a very capable scholar, well acquainted with such complexities of the language; in correspondence he quotes from a letter by a fellow cleric,

> At the head of the saints there stands Moses, whose face shone exceedingly, and was bright with the brightness of the sun...[31]

The solution to the enigma is offered through anthroposophical wisdom. That the two words in question are so similar, yet have such different meanings, is due to some awareness in previous ages, as the Hebrew language was being formed, that horns on animals' heads are formed by material substance condensing along the etheric streams, that rise up from (or descend down into) the animal's head. So these horns are in effect, making visible the shape of the etheric energies around the head. This linguistic fact here lends itself to the esoteric knowledge that the chakra in the forehead has two rays of light that stream out from the person. To conclude that Moses had this chakra activated, when he was in communion with his God, is very appropriate. As the scholar Mellinkoff points out, the idea that these 'horns' really meant 'rays of light' was the conclusion of a number of learned theologians in earlier times, such St. Gildas (6th century Britain), Rabbi Rashi (11th cent. France).[32]

**The Menorah-bush**
In the centre of this extraordinary scene, are those especially momentous words, written in Hebrew, which were spoken to Moses. They surround a central image, which unfortunately could not be made any clearer. This event in the life of Moses is extremely significant in this painting, because it is mirrored in the right side of the triptych, where the seven flames have become seven roses. We shall be exploring that scene in detail, later.

In a lecture about Moses, Rudolf Steiner endeavoured to explain to his audience how the divinity whom Moses encountered is the source of our higher-self; this divinity, is of course, referred to in translations of the Bible, as "God". But in the Hebrew the word used is "Elohim", and Rudolf Steiner explains that this term refers to a number of 'Powers' or sun-gods, usually the cosmic Christ or Jahveh. In the lecture about Moses, he refers to these deities as "the Cosmos Spirit". In various lectures he gave elsewhere about this encounter that Moses had, he identifies the Spirit addressing Moses as either the cosmic Christ or Jahve. Consequently, one can conclude that both these sublime beings were present, merged into the one being-ness, as it were.

Now that we have unveiled a sacred mystery of a Biblical text about the higher ego of human beings, there is even more to realize here, because in the painting, as we noted above, spreading out from the circle formed by the words spoken to Moses, are seven illumined branches. These represent the seven planets whose rays form the basis of the astral body, and below this are the twelve zodiac forces. These zodiacal energies form the basis of our ego-sense. In the lecture about the mission of Moses, Rudolf Steiner reveals the profound implications of what the Hebrew phrase is saying, and which is depicted in this scene,

> The human soul {can} feel that it exists dynamically within the {being and} activity of the Spiritual, just as the people of Egypt once felt {*where Moses lived, and was initiated*}. When a person feels with their inner being {*through attaining spiritual consciousness*} that they are in the midst of cosmic spiritual forces, then that soul shall feel that which manifested to Moses, for the first time ever, through clairvoyant consciousness {in the burning bush}. What is perceived then may be regarded as 'the Cosmos-Spirit'.

---

[31] The passage is from Bishop Salamis in Cyprus (in Letter LI) writing to Bishop John of Jerusalem; quoted in NPNF2-06, *The Principal Works of St. Jerome*, by Philip Schaff.

[32] R. Mellinkoff, *The Horned Moses, in Medieval Art and Thought*, Univ. of Calif, Press, 1970.

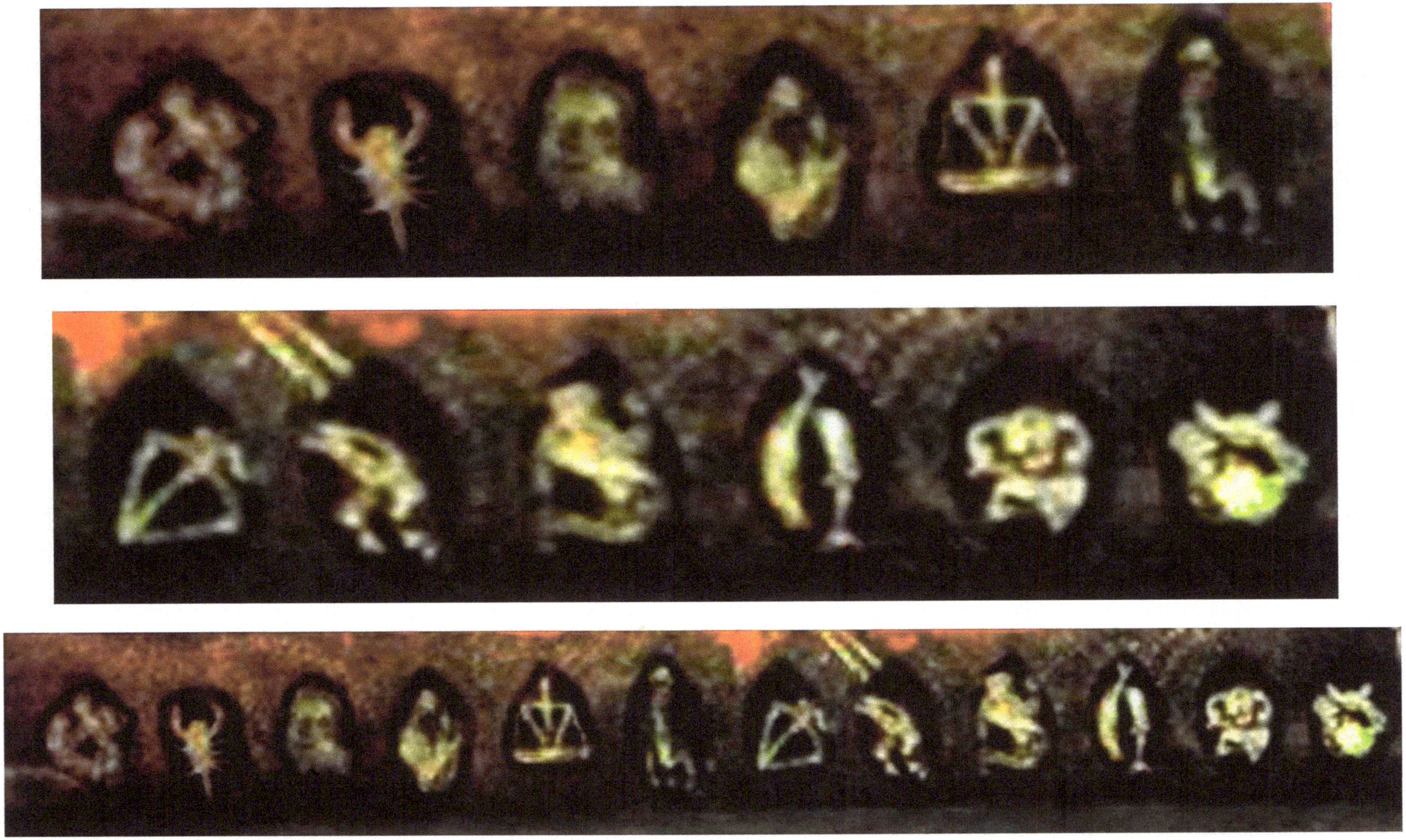

11 The zodiac beneath the 7-branched burning bush    Also shown above in two segments for clarity.

> And {*then one realizes*} just what it is that the various nations, through Moses, were given the impulse to move towards {*namely, the divine spiritual potential within oneself*}. And also through Moses, the capacity was assisted for a person to comprehend and experience this Cosmos-Spirit with their consciousness, as that Being who forms the underlying basis of the various elements that our world consists of.[33]

In these profound words, one finds the answer as to why the deity whom Moses experienced can be seen as the matrix of our own self. This is because we human beings are formed from the "underlying basis of the various elements that our world consists of". We are reminded here of how Rudolf Steiner refers to 'God' as the 'Weltengrund' (the foundational element of the cosmos). But what is the "underlying basis of the various elements that our world consists of"? This underlying basis is formed from: the seven planets and the zodiac. The zodiac is depicted here as an underlying element in this scene: it is depicted underneath the radiant 'menorah-bush', see illustration 11.

But now, in order to properly understand this scene – and to understand how it relates to its counterpart in the right side of the painting – it is important to note that we human beings generally don't have any awareness of the underlying cosmic bases to our consciousness. These planetary and zodiacal energies are active without the ego-sense of the person consciously integrating this. But the sublime consciousness of the divine beings of course encompasses and integrates this, and initiation could be regarded in part as striving towards this awareness.

**The zodiac under the menorah**
Now we need to explore the messages in this zodiac. Although these images are quite small, and therefore some of them were not clear on the photograph, we can learn some valuable esoteric truths from the unusual sequence seen here, see illustration 11. To do this, we need to know that a central theme in this huge painting is the life, or rather several lifetimes, of the holy initiate, Christian Rosencreutz. It is only this person who appears in all three sections of the painting. After Rudolf Steiner's death, as his students began to collate the wisdom contained in his vast output, and also learnt of comments made in private conversations. Through this it became possible to learn some veiled truths about the initiates who subtly assist humanity by working as intermediaries between the earthly world and divine beings in higher worlds who serve the Christ-impulse.

Rudolf Steiner revealed discreetly that Hiram, the master builder from about 1,000 BC, became the person known as Christian Rosencreutz in medieval Germany. But prior to incarnating in medieval times and becoming the founder of the Rosicrucian brotherhood, this great saint was incarnate at the time of Christ. In that century, he was the person known as 'Lazaros' (or 'Lazarus'), or rather Lazaros-John.[34] This became his name after the raising of Lazaros by Christ, an event which was a form of initiation, completed by Christ himself. As we shall see, Christian Rosencreutz appears in the right side of the painting and Lazaros-John appears in the central section.

**Gemini and Zarathustra**
Rudolf Steiner also revealed to a small group, that Lazaros has a spiritual link to the high initiate, Zarathustra[35]. Since Lazaros is the reincarnation of Hiram, it appears that here Hiram is representing the high initiate Zarathustra, who led the spiritual aspirations of people in the ancient Persian culture, which blossomed during the second Post-Atlantean Age (5067-2907 BC). This Age corresponds, in terms of the zodiac, to the Age of Gemini. We saw earlier that the zodiac shown above the scene in the Temple starts with Taurus, as the events around the building of Solomon's Temple occurred in the Age of Taurus. In a similar way, the zodiac under

---

[33] GA 60, p. 426.
[34] This incarnational sequence was discreetly revealed by Rudolf Steiner to intimate students, and is reported in GA 265, p. 420.
[35] GA 264, p.231.

the menorah, starting with Gemini, indicates that the events occurring with king Solomon and Hiram had their beginning in the Age of Gemini. In other words, the unusual starting point of this zodiac is saying that, it was in the Age of Gemini that Zarathustra stepped onto the world-stage and proclaimed the great cosmic Christ or sun-god, Ahura Mazdao, and this is the starting point of what is being depicted here with Hiram, who later became Lazaros.

**The images in the zodiac**
The actual images painted in this zodiac are somewhat unclear, but we can make some definite observations about them. We know that it starts with Gemini, because it ends at Taurus, and hence if one links up Taurus, the last sign, to the first, it has to be Gemini. The image is very blurred, but it appears to be of two people in a kind of playful interactive situation. Cancer is depicted as a sea-creature, a kind of lobster, rather than a crab. Leo appears to be depicted as a lion. Virgo comes next, but is very blurred, whether it is the traditional image of a deity holding some grain is not clear. Libra is next, and is a traditional set of scales. Scorpio is clearly depicted as a scorpion, facing downwards.

The next set of images starts with Sagittarius, which is depicted as an archer's bow. After this is Capricorn, but just what was painted here for Capricorn is not clear. The traditional image for Capricorn is a 'water-goat'; this image is possibly formed from legs of a goat, in the lower part, and above this, the head of a fish. The next image, that of Aquarius, is somewhat unclear, but it is based on a water deity letting some water cascade downwards. Next is a clear depiction of two fishes, for Pisces. Then for Aries one can see with some difficulty, a ram looking directly at the viewer. Finally, for Taurus there is an unclear but definite drawing of a bull, looking over towards its left side.

**Capricorn and the energy lines**
There is an additional feature here, connected with the sign of Capricorn. There are two lines of energy coming from the central part of the menorah down to Capricorn. This feature gives a prominence to Capricorn. The central part of the menorah has of course the words from Jahve-Christ, so this feature indicates something about the Christ reality. The veiled meaning of this feature appears to be that Jesus, who is destined to be the vessel of Christ, shall be born in the month of Capricorn, which he was, in late December. Later, we shall discover that there is another esoteric meaning indicated here.

**The Ark of the Covenant**
Looking at the upper section of the left side of the painting, above the zodiac encompassing the three people inside Solomon's Temple, is the Ark of the Covenant, see illustration 12. In the Book of Deuteronomy, Chapter 10, it is described how God (understood in anthroposophy to be Jahweh-Christ) commanded Moses to create a wooden box (or Ark) and to deposit in it the stone tablets of the Ten Commandments. Later Jewish traditions understood that the Ark also contained, as the Epistle to the Hebrews reports, a golden jar of manna (the miraculous food that nourished the Israelites in their wanderings) and the staff of Aaron that budded and produced almonds when God needed to establish which of the twelve tribes was to become the priestly tribe. So the Ark came to represent the divine will of God to the Hebrews. In esoteric terms it functioned as a kind of portal which gave divine beings access to the Hebrew people, through its proximity to the priests in the temple. Hence here in the painting, the Ark is permeated by divine energies streaming forth from the highest feature of the entire painting, namely the radiant triangle in the centre of the picture, which symbolizes the Divine, or God.

But also the Ark is shown here with the two Cherubim that are thought of as its guardian spirits. However, historically there is no definite mention of the Ark having these two spiritual guardians, until some three centuries after Moses. This occurred when King Solomon had carvings of these two spiritual beings made and then installed on the Ark, when he moved it from a temporary location into the Holy of Holies inside his new (actual) temple. So once again, this feature refers to King Solomon's temple, emphasizing that **the task of building the spiritual**

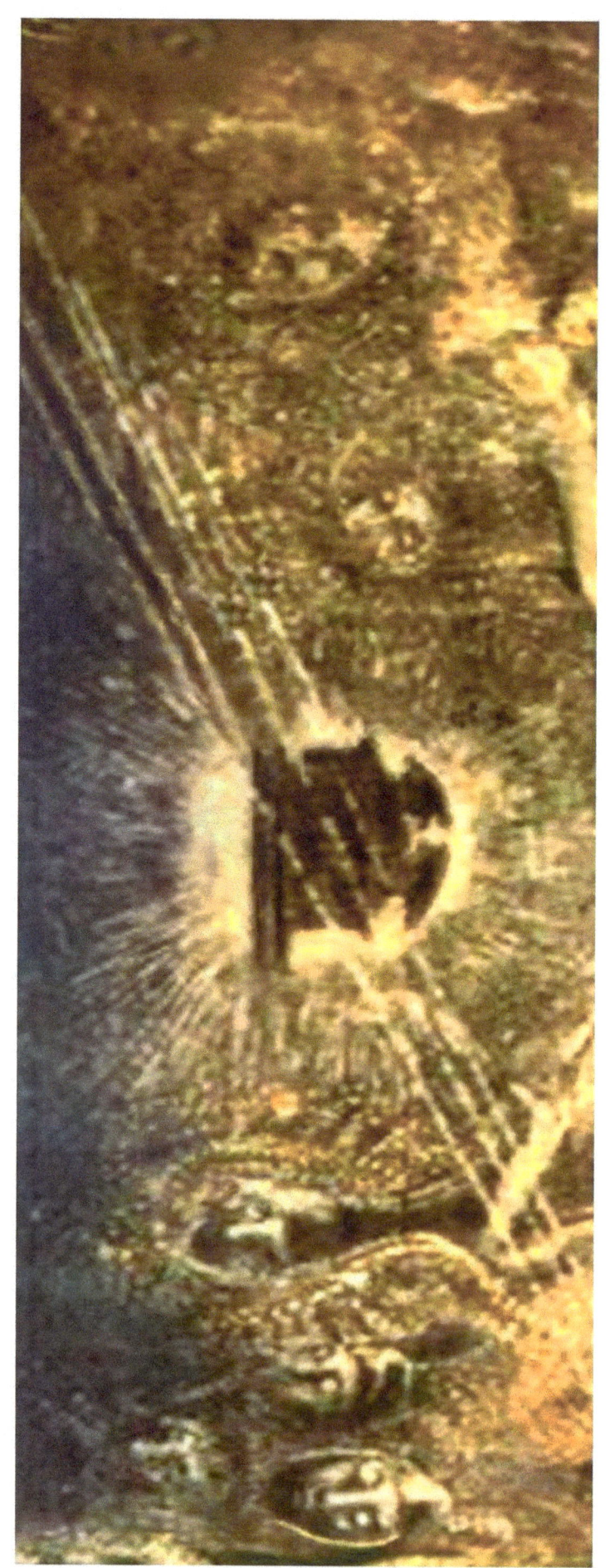

12 The Ark of the Covenant for Solomon's temple, and inspiring Angels

**temple, the vessel for our future Spiritual-self**, the Masonic theme of Solomon's Temple, is the focus of this scene.

### The Angels of the pre-Golgotha Mysteries

To either side of the Ark several spiritual beings are depicted, possibly seven in total, see illustration 12. But on the right side of the painting, in the counterpart to this area, there are no such beings, as the area to the left and right of the dove are empty. This feature tells the viewer that in the cultural epochs prior to the Greco-Latin Age, the so-called 'semi-gods' were the teachers of humanity, who appeared to the priests in various ancient Mystery centres. The learned ancient Egyptian writer Manetho, who may have been a priest at the very significant centre of Heliopolis, recorded this tradition of semi-gods, which is confirmed by Rudolf Steiner.

The historically more recent reverence for Krishna and for Mithra is a special, later example of this kind of inspiring work from the spiritual worlds. For both of these movements derive from reverence for a divine being; in fact, for the influence of he who would become known as Jesus of Nazareth, but about 1,000 years before his actual incarnation. He was in these situations therefore active as a kind of divine semi-god being, in whom higher Powers were also operative.

The Angels who inspired the people associated with various Mysteries, and referred to as semi-gods, were of several kinds. They were either divine (that is, normally evolved) angelic beings, or somewhat less evolved Angels, or luciferic Angels: all had their specific missions to carry out with humanity.

We can now contemplate the central middle section of the painting.

# The Middle Section

## Jachin and Boaz

Before we can effectively contemplate the scenes in the central area and over on the right side of the painting, we need to understand the upper area, which, like the lower area, is also divided by the two large columns. At the top of these columns are two beings, which Anna May's pamphlet tells us are Zeitgeister or Principalities. It is the Principalities who become the Regents of the cultural epochs such as the post-Atlantean Ages, each of which lasts for 2,160 years. But before we consider these two columns as the two Time-Spirits, we need to bear in mind that every Masonic temple follows the Bible description of Solomon's temple, which states that it had two columns prominently placed in it. Today every Masonic temple has two columns inside, or just outside, the entrance. In the description of Solomon's temple, these two columns are given the Hebrew names of Jachin and Boaz. A meditative verse by Rudolf Steiner gives much insight into what these symbolize, and how they represent the nature of what king Solomon and Hiram symbolize in the painting,

> JACHIN   (wisdom, Solomon)
> In pure thinking you find the self which
> can maintain its own being.
> When you transform the thought into an image
> you can experience the creative wisdom.

Jachin is then, about the meditative path that leads to receiving wisdom into the soul. By contrast, this is what Solomon represents in the painting,

> BOAZ   (activity/strength, Hiram)
> When you condense feeling to light,
> then you make manifest the Formative Power.
> When you make the Will material in an object
> you then are creating, in cosmic existence.

This verse is quite enigmatic, but one can see that it is about taking the path of being actively involved in transforming the material world, and achieving skill and insights. Lines three and four are actually saying,

> When you put your will into the material world – for higher purposes –
> then you are being creative as part of the cosmic reality.

Looking again at the first verse, the one for Jachin, we find that it is less enigmatic over-all, but it is important to realize that lines three and four are actually saying:

> When you can go beyond an idea (which is a mental image) for a project, and attain the state of sensing the vibrant astral image or living thought-form behind the earthly thought, then you can undertake your work out of a living, creative wisdom.

So Boaz is the other pathway, where direct interaction in the material world gradually brings about wisdom and skills. This is what Hiram Abiff represents in the painting (as well as being also a real historical person). We should note at this point that the painting actually does have two columns in it, even though they do not resemble the carved columns used in a temple or in a freemason lodge. These are the two 'columns', on either side of the crucifixion scene which divide the painting into three sections, making it a triptych. We shall be exploring these in detail, later.

## The two columns in the painting

In the painting, the two Time-Spirits have a deeply impressive quality, radiating power and majesty. Here is an extract of what Anna May wrote about these beings in her pamphlet for visitors to the Glass Palace exhibition in Munich. I have added a few explanatory words to her abbreviated way of writing,

> The upper part of The Triptych Grail presents the spiritual world, gold {in colour}; the highest, largest heads: the Time Spirits (*Archai*), who extend out their hands over large epochs, succeeding each other in sequence. Supporting these beings are the Folk-spirits (Archangels). Beneath these beings are the *Angeloi* or Angels, gazing down onto humanity.

Looking at the painting, we can see the arms of each of the Time Spirits or Principalities, extending out, and their hands are grasped by a hand from another Principality at the very top of the left and right of the painting, where it begins to curve downwards. Of these additional Principalities only a hand is in the picture. But underneath where these hands meet, are two Archangels whose arms are bent directly upwards, supporting the meeting of the hands of two Time Spirits. This feature indicates interaction of the Archangels with the Principalities. This interaction is significant, but before we explore that, we need to identify who these two Principalities are, and thus which zodiac Age each governs.

**The left column and the Egyptian Time-Spirit**
The column on the left side of the Christ-deed – the left side here indicates a time before the Mystery of Golgotha – depicts a mighty being whom we could call 'Pharao', see illustration 12. This is the Time-spirit or Principality who was the Folk-spirit of ancient Egypt, but whom during the Age of Taurus (the Third Post-Atlantean Age), became the Regent of that Age, which we call the Mesopotamian-Egyptian cultural epoch (lasting from 2907 to 747 BC). The column on the right side of the Christ-deed – indicating a time after the Mystery of Golgotha – depicts the mighty being whom we could call 'Hellas', see illustration 13. This is the Time-spirit or Principality who was the Folk-spirit of ancient Greece, but who during the Age of Aries (the Fourth Post-Atlantean Age), became the Regent of that Age, which we call the Greco-Latin cultural epoch (from 747 BC to AD 1413).

How can we conclude that these two Principalities are those who relate to these two Ages? Rudolf Steiner has indicated this by the head-dress of the two beings. The being on the left is firstly, active prior to the Mystery of Golgotha, and that can only refer to the Ancient Indian, ancient Persian or Mesopotamian-Egyptian cultural epochs. But of these, only the Mesopotamian-Egyptian cultural epoch is immediately next to the Christ-event, apart from the Greco-Latin age, (which extends beyond the Golgotha events) so this Time-spirit appears to be "Pharao". A further indication is the head-dress on this being, which has two elements of the ancient Egyptian culture.

One is the hair-style of this being, it reminds one of both the 'Nemes' cloth head-dress of Egyptian Pharaohs, and also of the straight long wigs used by high-ranking Egyptians to protect their shaven heads from the intense sun. The other indicators are the two angled leaf-like shapes on the head, which remind one of the typical Egyptian 'palmette' architectural column. Whereas the Time-spirit in the right pillar has a head-dress which has scroll-shapes, and these are very reminiscent of the 'volutes' that adorn the upper part of the Grecian Ionic column; for examples of all these, see illustration 15.

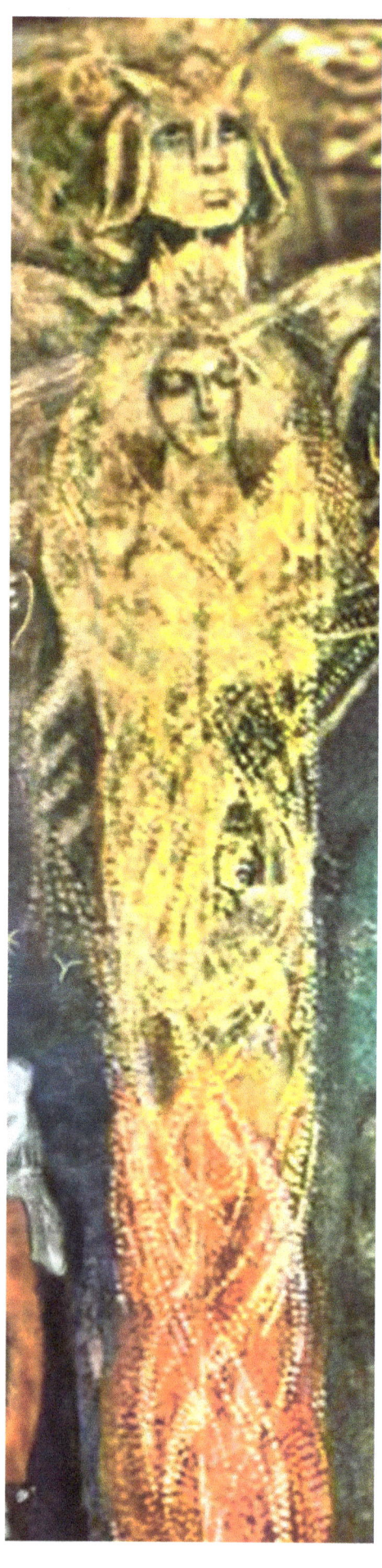

**13  The left column: the majestic Time-Spirit (an Archai) 'Pharao'**

Below is the Buddha, his aura formed and permeated by various resplendent spiritual energies.

Further below, with closed eyes is an acolyte representing the old initiation process in which the ego-sense was repressed.

**14 The Right column: The majestic Time-Spirit (an Archai) 'Hellas'**

Below is Lazaros-John, holding the Earth with a cross, symbolizing both the cosmic Christ as the Earth-Spirit and the process of 'taking up one's cross'.

Further below, with open eyes, is an acolyte who represents the new initiation process in which the ego-sense is to be maintained, but spiritualized.

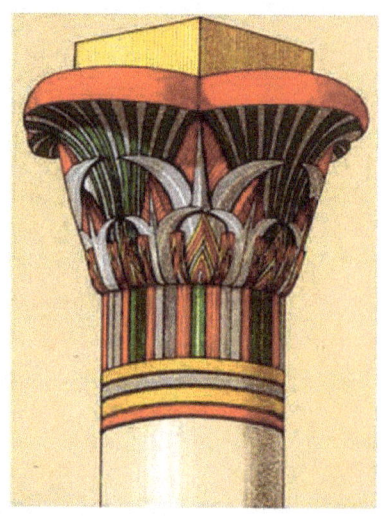 

## 15 Egyptian & Grecian artistic styles
Above, top: two versions of Egyptian 'palmette' columns.
Above, lower: two Egyptian head gear.

Below: two examples of Grecian 'Ionic' columns

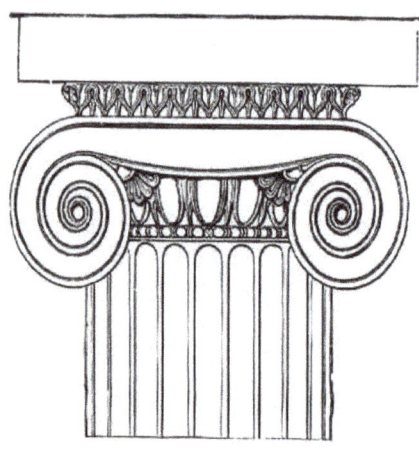 

**The right column & the Greek Time-spirit**
It can appear at first that my identification of these two beings is incorrect because 'Hellas', or the Time-spirit of the Greco-Latin Age, is placed on the post-Golgotha side of the picture, whereas in fact this Age began already in 747 BC. However, it is the case that the two hands of the great Principalities meet above the cross, as if to suggest that the Age of Taurus ended, and the Age of Aries began, right at AD 33. But, actually this is not historically the case; it was in 747 BC that these two Ages met. So the time-sequence of these two Principalities in regard to the Christ-event, that is, the end of one Age and the beginning of the next, is not being portrayed literally here. Likewise the Time-Spirit Hellas, is located on the right side of the cross, even though that Age began in 747 BC; but this is precisely correct because 'Hellas' did not begin his reign as Time-spirit until after the Golgotha events; this was about the 1st or 2nd century AD.

Rudolf Steiner explains that the archangel who was the Folk-spirit of ancient Greece surrendered his guiding role over the Greeks, and became the Time-spirit of the Greco-Latin Age. In that role this being, raised to the rank of Principality, could assist the spread of exoteric Christianity, becoming the guiding spirit of Christianity, as the Gospel was being proclaimed in the early centuries, mainly through the common Greek language. Hence the arm of 'Hellas' that extends towards the cross is thick and solid, indicating that this Time-Spirit is directly inspired by, or is deeply linked to, the Christ-impulse. Whereas the left arm of 'Pharao' thins out as it extends towards the Golgotha-events, for this Age dies out prior to the coming of Christ.

We notice too, how the area around the outstretched left arm of 'Pharao' is quite dark, in comparison to that of the right arm of 'Hellas'; this indicates the gradual loss of spiritual light in the earthly sphere, in the centuries leading up the time of Christ. There had been a gradual build up of astral darkness due to the influence of Lucifer and Ahriman gaining more power in human consciousness, making the possibility of initiation more difficult, and leading to the beginning of materialism. Human souls after death were also becoming less empowered, and hence caught in a darkened astral sphere around the Earth.

**Novalis: Hymn to the Night**
The great German poet, Novalis, inspired by initiatory insights, referred to this in his magnificent poems, *The Hymns to the Night*. In the *Fifth Hymn to the Night*, Novalis refers subtly to the Grecian Folk-spirit, who shall shortly take on the role of becoming the guiding spirit of Christianity. The song of this spiritual-being focuses on the profound mystery of how the sacrifice of Christ allows a human soul to develop a higher self, which preserves and enhances their self-consciousness in the spiritual realms after life has ended.

> From distant shores, born under the radiant skies of Hellas, a singer came to Palestine,
> and offered all of his heart to the wondrous child (singing:)
> "The youth art thou, who since long ages has stood on our gravestones, immersed in thought immense: a comforting sign in the darkness – the joyous beginning of the higher humanity. What has placed us into deep sadness, now draws us with sweet yearning from here. In death was Life-Eternal announced, and Thou art death, who makest us be healed".[36]          (Translated, the author)

These words of Novalis about 'Hellas' in relation to Christ are especially relevant here for several reasons. The deed of Christ has much to do with offering a solution to the problem of death; and as Rudolf Steiner pointed out, death was far more disconcerting to the people in the Greco-Latin Age than to people in any earlier Age. For by that Age the soul, when incarnate, was more deeply immersed in the physical world than in earlier times. Also the death on the cross, the sacrifice by Christ, is graphically depicted here and this event is the pivotal point of the entire painting. But before we contemplate this theme, let's consider the two faces below the Principalities in these columns. To do this, we need to regard the space above these two smaller persons, which has the two Principalities, as belonging to a different part of the painting. These two smaller faces relate to a different theme, and to a different sequence of time. The person in the left side column is,

---

[36] Novalis, Band 1, *Das dichterische Werk, Tagebücher und Briefe*, edit. R. Samuel, C. Handser Vlg, Munich, 1978.

as Anna May reports, the Buddha, whereas the person in the right side column, under 'Hellas', is Lazaros-John. He is holding the Earth on which is a cross, we shall explore the significance of that below.

Buddha is placed here to represent the last of the great initiates of the pre-Christian era. Lazaros-John is depicted to represent the first of the initiates appearing after the Golgotha events. But Lazaros-John is also here because, as Rudolf Steiner revealed in more private circles, Hiram incarnated again at the time of Christ, and became this elect person, who was initiated by Christ, in the 'raising of Lazaros'.

Underneath each of these men is a smaller face. The person underneath Buddha has his eyes closed because, as Anna May indicated in her pamphlet, the pre-Christian acolytes were initiated in a manner that was not using the conscious ego-sense; instead the acolyte was put into a kind of sleep state for three days. By contrast, the person underneath Lazaros-John has his eyes open, because as new initiates arise in the post-Golgotha era, they shall be aware of what is developing in their consciousness; that is, their ego-sense shall be retained in the process of developing the higher ego.

**The World-Cross: Plato and the enchanted Deity**
That Lazaros-John is holding a globe with a cross within it, can be seen as representing the Earth as belonging to Christ, emphasizing that the great sun god has become the Spirit of the Earth. But there is another meaning here, which is about the 'world-cross' and an esoteric statement from Plato about the Divine as embodied within the world, with its fourfold structure, as Rudolf Steiner explained in 1902:

> In the cross we have the same concept as we have in the philosophy of Plato, in which the All-Spirit {Soul of the World} is crucified {in the fourfold material world.}[37]

Rudolf Steiner often directly or indirectly referred to this idea in his teachings. On one occasion he explains that the cross itself represents the four elements (and associated etheric forces). He points out that this is why the short inscription, written by Pontius Pilate was placed on the cross. In the Rosicrucian inspired Isenheim Altarpiece, this is painted with just the four letters JNRJ. Rudolf Steiner explains that these four letters represent the four elements, being the first letters in Hebrew, of water, fire, air and earth.[38] In the Anna May painting, the small inscription is there, but the words or letters are not shown.

The statement from Plato about the world-soul is in his *Timaeus* (Sections 33 & 34) and is somewhat complex, as the Greek text is ambiguous in places and quite abrupt. Plato is explaining here the spatial and geometrical aspects of how Creation came about. It is in the process of this, that he presents the profoundly potent idea of the Divine Spirit existing within, or rather, discreetly behind, the physical universe (probably in effect, the solar system). This Spirit or Soul of the Cosmos, is put there by the First Deity (the Father God, in Christian terms). He begins section 34 saying,

> Such was the over-all plan of the eternal God {'Reason-endowed Deity'}, about the God then coming-into-being {'reasoning Deity'} {for whom he made} a smooth and even body, having a surface in every direction.....and in the centre {the Sun} he put Soul and spread this out throughout the entirety {of creation}...          (trans. the author)

To the ancient Greeks, divine beings, as distinct from nature spirits and other similar entities, were endowed with spiritual consciousness or high cosmic intelligence; they used the word 'reason' for such divine beings. Here Plato is teaching that the second deity would also manifest such cosmic intelligence, but not to such a degree as the Father-god, but its powers of

---

[37] Archive lecture, 1st Mar.1902, Berlin.
[38] Earth *Jabasch*, Fire *nur*, Air *ruach*, Water *Iam*.

consciousness would increase with time.[39] Although his language is obscure, one sees the idea being presented here is that, implicit within the physical world, interwoven in the different nature realms, is the Divine: an idea which is defined as "panentheism'". Although Plato does not state it here, the implication is also that eventually, from the secondary deity, (the Soul of the Cosmos), humanity will emerge, and within humanity this great Soul of the Cosmos will be slumbering. This teaching has similarities to the 'Logos' idea in St. John's Gospel, which derives from the Father God, and from whom all things in turn have been created in particular, humanity. Within the human being, the Logos is slumbering. In addition, in a later paragraph, Plato refers to Creation as having an "X" shape, or fourfold shape which is a cross shape, although on an angle.

**Rudolf Steiner and the Word-Cross**

Very early Christian writers, perceiving this, saw a resonance between their religion, wherein Jesus was crucified on a cross, and Plato's very influential idea, by pointing out that Plato had taught that the divine Soul of the World was 'crucified' on a (world-)cross.[40] Rudolf Steiner agreed with this conclusion, and gave a deeper understanding of this by explaining that the concept behind Plato's words leads to a profound realization of the four realms of existence: mineral, plant, animal and human, as graded manifestations of 'God', that is, of divine beings as they manifest the creative intentions of the Logos, who is the vessel of the Father-god. In other words, the Divine is present in a dulled down way in the mineral realm, but stirs in the plants, arises to a dream-like state in the astral dynamics of the animals and awakens in humanity, with its sense of self.

Rudolf Steiner made many references to this perception, and used it directly or subtly in his lectures, and in his meditation verses, especially those from 1924. The especial relevance for the spiritual seeker of this idea from Plato is that the path to self-initiation is in effect a path that awakens the higher ego: awakens the divine within the earthly ego.

Rudolf Steiner also explained that the meaning behind the admonition of Christ, "Take up your cross and follow me", is directly related to the deep revelation of Plato that Divine being-ness is placed within the fourfold Creation. To understand this profound feature in the painting by Anna May, we need to consider this Gospel statement in its context. In the Gospel of St. Matthew, (16:24-25), just after the words about the cross, Jesus speaks of the requirement for those who seek initiation to rise above the earthly, partially illusory Self.

> Then Jesus said to his disciples, "If anyone would come after me, he must disown himself and take up his cross and follow me.
> For whoever wills to safely preserve his soul shall nullify it {shall have it pass away}, but whoever nullifies their soul for my sake, shall encounter it."

Rudolf Steiner taught that this statement about taking up one's cross, (also found in St. Mark, 8:34 & St. Luke, 9:23) is about the fourfold cross as the fourfold earthly world, and that the small wooden bar with an inscription "INRI" on it, which Pontius Pilate arranged to have placed on the cross, refers to the four ethers, and hence the four states of matter. He explains that when Jesus was placed on the cross then – in an awe-inspiring echo of the esoteric truth preserved by Plato – the Divine was stretched out on, or caught by, the fourfold material world. But the intention of the gods in creating humanity, and placing human beings within the physical fourfold world, is that the higher triad, of Spirit-self, Life-spirit and Spirit-human, can be brought into being, through our incarnations in this environment.[41]

---

[39] This subtle distinction between the two deities is expressed by Plato using a word for this second being which is a passive participle (logistheis, λογισθείς), rather than the noun, 'reason' (logismos, λογισμός) In Plato's Greek: Οὗτος δὴ πᾶς ὄντος ἀεὶ λογισμος Θεου περὶ τὸν ποτὲ ἐσόμενον Θεον λογισθεὶς λειον;

[40] Justin Martyr, in *Apol. 1*, para. 60 and Irenaeus of Lyons in, *The Proof of Apostolic Preaching*.

[41] Lecture, 29th May 1905, and notes of an esoteric session, 28th Nov. 1906.

In an esoteric lesson he taught that the process of building up humanity through the aeons and through the mineral, plant and animals stages is a process of the world forming the ego-sense from 'outside to the inside', whereas the Divine, through the deed of Christ, seeks to build the higher ego-sense from the 'inside to the outside'. In other words, in the first case the external world, over aeons, has been building up the fourfold nature, to allow a human being to arise. Whereas in the latter case, the Divine prompts the human being to develop his or her divine potential from within outwards, thereby gaining mastery over the mineral, etheric and astral realms.

**The Crucifixion Scene**
With the Crucifixion scene, this painting takes us into the most sacred of all the many themes illumined by Rudolf Steiner's spiritual wisdom and research. Here we cannot present more than an outline of what he revealed about the significance of Christ and the events which occurred on Golgotha hill. The reader is referred to Rudolf Steiner's many lectures for a more comprehensive understanding of this subject. But here we can remind ourselves that the core aspect of esoteric Christianity as taught by Rudolf Steiner, is that the cosmic Christ being descended from spiritual realms 'behind' the physical sun, and united to the Earth's aura. But before we explore this, it may be helpful to review briefly the esoteric perspective on Christianity that Rudolf Steiner has offered. As I wrote in *the Rudolf Steiner Handbook,* a good introduction to Rudolf Steiner's teachings on this subject is found in his book, *Christianity as Mystical Fact.* And a good place to start with his teachings on Christianity is his statement which has the quality of a Zen Buddhist 'koan',

> Christianity began as a religion, but is greater than all religions, including Christianity.

In other words, what we know (or, don't truly know) as Christianity, is in fact something else, something which transcends the formal structure of a religion. Rudolf Steiner's perspective here is that the scriptures of this religion present a sacred narrative, but they also veil a profound cosmic event, understanding of which requires initiation wisdom. So what is then the core difference in Rudolf Steiner's esoteric Christianity to that of the churches today? It is the difference between 'Jesus' and 'Christ'.

Rudolf Steiner taught that there is a cosmic deity overshadowing Jesus. And obviously a deity is a different kind of being to a human, even a most sacred human being. In anthroposophy, the term 'Christ', when strictly used, refers to the cosmic being who came upon (or, 'anointed') Jesus at the Baptism in the Jordan River. So in anthroposophy, the person known as 'Jesus Christ' is a being consisting of the man Jesus, and also of the deity, the Christ being, who became present in him, as from the Baptism. This viewpoint of two distinct but deeply interlinked entities being involved was held by earlier Christians, including the great Origenes of Alexandria, but later this view was condemned as a heresy.[42] However, as we shall see, it is also understood in anthroposophy that the person Jesus, after the Baptism in the River Jordan, became eternally united to the cosmic deity, becoming the archetype of what future humanity is to evolve towards. (We shall return to this theme, below). To Rudolf Steiner, Jesus was of immense sanctity; and he taught that for a person to be Christian, she or he needs to consciously make a sincere inner decision to be someone who regards Christ as their Saviour.

So in Rudolf Steiner's anthroposophy, the deed of the cosmic Christ occurring on Golgotha hill at Jerusalem, is understood to have resulted in a permeation of the aura of the Earth with sacred spiritual energies. As Jesus died on the cross, the great deity illumining him, the cosmic Christ, merged its own divine etheric and astral auras with the aura of our planet, with mother Earth. Rudolf Steiner describes this event as the most sacred and important event in the lifespan of the planet. This event resulted in a radiant spiritual light permanently imbuing our planet; a light from which our Spirit-Self, and the Life-Spirit, derives. Rudolf Steiner describes how to the

---

[42] Adoptionism, identified as starting with Theodotus in 190 AD, is one form of this awareness; Monophysitism (associated with Eutyches (378-454) is another, and Apollinarianism (Syria 4th cent.) is another.

**16 The Crucifixion**: With Joseph of Arimathea and the Archangel Michael are a group of witnesses, all of whom are spirit beings.

modern initiate, this event can be seen as if from far out in space. The seer then observes new glorious radiance, in the shape of a star, arising in the Earth's own aura.¹

**Christ as the Spirit of the Earth**
Now to make clear that this union of the cosmic Christ with the Earth is a core spiritual truth, and hence emphasized by Rudolf Steiner, we need to consider the overall context of this truth, in its cultural and religious context. As I wrote in *The Hellenistic Mysteries and Christianity*, Rudolf Steiner emphasized that the word 'Christ' refers to a cosmic or divine being, whereas the word 'Jesus' refers to a human being, although an immensely holy person. In his view of Christianity, the cosmic Christ is the core deity and his teachings are the most profound available on this theme.

It is central to his view that the cosmic Christ became united to the Earth (to its aura or soul) at the time of the Crucifixion of Jesus. He often emphasized that the Earth became the body of the deity, Christ. To offer as Biblical evidence for this, a verse from the Gospel of St. John was referred to, as providing affirmation, if not precisely proof, of his teaching on this theme. The verse used by him is John 13:18, and in English translations of his lectures one finds him quoting this verse in this way, "Those who eat my bread, tread on me with their feet."

But such a translation of the Greek sentence has perplexed students of anthroposophy over the years, because the normal, historical level of meaning here obviously concerns hostility from Judas Iscariot. In the English versions it appears as, **"The one eating my bread, he has lifted-up his heel against me"**. The meaning here is of course that Judas has become antagonistic to Jesus. In the Martin Luther version it appears as, **"He who eats my bread, is trampling on me."** This version means that Judas is regarded as metaphorically trampling on Jesus. But to make it into something positive, involves dismantling the German idiom to trample, and reading it 'to harmlessly walk upon'.

But when a deeper level of meaning in the sacred text is accessed, we see it is hinting that people, in digesting plant foods are in effect absorbing energies from Christ. Because the verb used here means to really digest living (plant-based) food, but yet it is only ever used by St. John regarding absorbing or receiving into oneself, the light of Christ. So it means that people can absorb life-filled nourishment from Christ. That points us to the subtle life-forces of the planet, and to the presence of Christ in these. This initiatory or inspired level of meaning in the gospel also then is in harmony with such other words of Christ, as "I am the bread of life".

And the people who are doing this, they are all incarnate people, because they are walking along over the Earth. Lastly, human beings, in walking along across the planet, are walking across Christ (not Jesus). John 13:18 is saying that soon people shall be walking over Christ, absorbing the life-forces of the great cosmic god, because He shall soon become the indwelling guiding spirit of the planet.

To point towards this layer of meaning, Rudolf Steiner has used Luther's translation because Luther's German idiom for trampling is literally, "....tread on me with their feet". By taking this idiom literally, one can take a kind of short-cut to the third level of

---

[43] This is mentioned in many lectures; e.g., in GA 104, lect. 23 June 1908.

meaning, since it points to people walking along. And this was no doubt an appropriate decision by Rudolf Steiner at the time, and for his purposes.[44]

In *The Hellenistic Mysteries and Christianity,* I established in detail the accuracy of Steiner's translation, showing that the deepest meaning of the sophisticated Greek grammar used in John 13:18 accords fully with Rudolf Steiner's explanation, and confirms his understanding of a merging of the deity with the planet. For hidden in the inspired Greek words of the Gospel is the following meaning:

> **Those who are consuming living plant foods**
> **are eating that which belongs to me;**
> **and those same persons are walking and those**
> **same persons are walking across me.** (St. John 13:18)

Rudolf Steiner expressed this esoteric Christian truth in a powerful, concise manner during a 1909 lecture,

> Through the event that we call the Mystery of Golgotha, or in other words, the walking of Christ upon the Earth, that spiritual being who was previously within the sun, united itself to the Earth. And that humanity has divided the flow of time into 'before-Christ' {BC} and 'after-Christ' {AD} has its basis in the situation that, this living being who we call the Earth, actually went through an important development. What was previously only to be found on the sun, is since then to be found in the astral aura of the Earth.... In the events of Golgotha the {cosmic} Christ-spirit has united with the Earth.[45]

Rudolf Steiner taught that the sacrificial death on Golgotha hill, extended beyond that of the most holy man, Jesus of Nazareth, and encompassed, as a profound sacrifice, an Archangelic being. That is, apart from the great Sun-god, the cosmic Christ, there was also present in the events on Golgotha, an Archangel; a being who was an especial vessel of the cosmic Christ-impulse within the hierarchy of the archangels. The holiness of the Golgotha events surpasses the power of language to portray, in terms of both the sacrifice made out of love for humanity, and the decisiveness of the change brought about for humanity's future, because of the in-dwelling of the cosmic Christ in the Earth's soul.

But we can draw upon the epistles of St. Paul, the poems of Novalis, and the many lectures and meditative verses by Rudolf Steiner, to immerse the soul in contemplation of these truths. We shall return to this theme when contemplating the experience of St. Paul on the road to Damascus, depicted in the right section of the painting, because it is the union of the cosmic Christ with the Earth that has made possible the third section of the triptych. The development of a high spirituality, such as the third section depicts, is dependent upon the presence of the Christ light in the Earth's aura.

The depiction of the Golgotha event here has an awe-inspiring, evocative quality due to many features, but in particular this quality is created by the lower section, which depicts the blood of the Redeemer flowing inside the Earth, see illustration 16. Another striking feature, adding to the power of this scene, is that the group of witnesses gathered behind the cross are, with one exception, all spiritual beings, not human beings. Consequently the event, whilst treated as a physical reality, is also being depicted from the viewpoint of a spiritual entity, or a clairvoyant person. As a result, instead of an area of darkness enveloping the cross, as in Matthias Grünewald's masterpiece, the *Isenheim Altarpiece* (another Rosicrucian-initiate inspired painting), here we see a golden-yellow auric glow around the body of Jesus. This indicates the

---

[44] In In 1908, Steiner faced a question after a lecture as to why he insisted that this sentence in John 13:18 revealed that a cosmic Christ being would unite to the Earth, when "obviously the Greek did not say that". In English, it is my recollection that he replied: it is a shame that this has not been seen correctly, but in the future someone shall appear who shall establish that this sentence does refer to the union of Christ to the Earth." ( Frag.-Beantw. #1789)

[45] GA 108, p. 86, lecture 17th Jan. 1909.

presence of the cosmic sun-god Christ, whose sublime spiritual nature is about to permeate the Earth's aura.

## A crowd of witnesses

Gathered around, as a crowd of witnesses, are about 20 entities, the only one of these which can be identified is the Archangel Michael, who is seen on the right side of the scene, holding his sword down towards the Earth's interior. This affirms the accuracy of the knowledge incorporated in an early Christian apocryphal text, *The Questions of Bartholomew*, portraying a dialogue between the risen Christ and the disciple Bartholomew:

> And Bartholomew said: "Lord, when Thou went to be hung upon the cross, I followed Thee afar off, and saw Thee hung on the cross, and I saw the Angels coming down from Heaven and worshipping Thee. And then there came darkness; I beheld, and I saw that thou wast vanished away under the cross, and I heard only a voice in the Earth's interior....Tell me, Lord, whither wentest thou from the cross?"
> And Jesus answered and said: "Blessed art thou Bartholomew my beloved one, because thou sawest this Mystery... when I vanished away from the cross, then I went down into Hades that I might bring up Adam and all that were with him, according to the plea of Archangel Michael". Then, the ascent of Adam up out of Hades is seen, he was borne aloft by Angels.... Again Bartholomew said: "Lord, I saw the Angels ascending before Adam and singing praises. But one of the Angels, which was {a} very great {being}, superior to the rest of the Angels, would not ascend up with them; and there was in his hand, a sword of fire, and he was gazing steadfastly at Thee only. And all the Angels besought him to arise with him, but he would not".[46]

It is of course, a primary truth in anthroposophy that this Archangel is an especially significant member of the hosts of divine beings around the cosmic Christ. He was known as the 'countenance of Jahve' in Old Testament times. Rudolf Steiner's uniquely profound insights into the Christ Mysteries will be in part due to his deep spiritual rapport with this Archangel. In the painting by Anna May we see two profound depictions of this truth. One is the unusual 'Tree of Life' extending up beyond the cross, and the other is the scene occurring down inside the Earth.

## The Subterranean world

What does the subterranean scene wish to convey? Anna May wrote about this in her brief pamphlet, from her own understanding (which is not necessarily always correct), and perhaps also reflecting words spoken to her by Rudolf Steiner. But in her text it is not clear whether there are any statements from Rudolf Steiner embedded in her text,

> ...the holy blood of Golgotha, which penetrates the Earth, and which is taken up by 'The Mothers', who are the three earth-forces of thinking, feeling and will. With Christ, the Sun god, {other} spiritual beings came also down to the Earth, who also work with this blood, so that the blood permeates these three forces and makes them Christ-permeated.

Let us now contemplate this scene. We see the blood of Jesus, representing the presence of the cosmic Christ, falling onto the ground and then, astonishingly, dripping down inside the Earth, to be caught up by three mysterious dark figures; see illustration 17. It is of course important to realize that no actual physical blood drips down inside the Earth, although some physical blood may well have dripped into the soil. But inside the Earth, it is entirely symbolic of the spiritual forces of the cosmic Christ. However as it is still being depicted as blood, this instructs the viewer firstly to remember that blood is the vessel of the astral energies. Secondly, it is teaching that within the astral body or soul of Jesus, the divine cosmic Christ was present; and thirdly that within our soul, and hence own bloodstream, these same forces are to become present, although to a much lesser degree.

The scene here is better understood if we view it in the light of the wisdom of various esoteric traditions. There is the cultural past of Germany, derived from the ancient Druidic mystery

---

[46] Published in "*The Apocryphal New Testament*", p. 166 - 186, edit. M. R. James, Oxford UP, 1975.

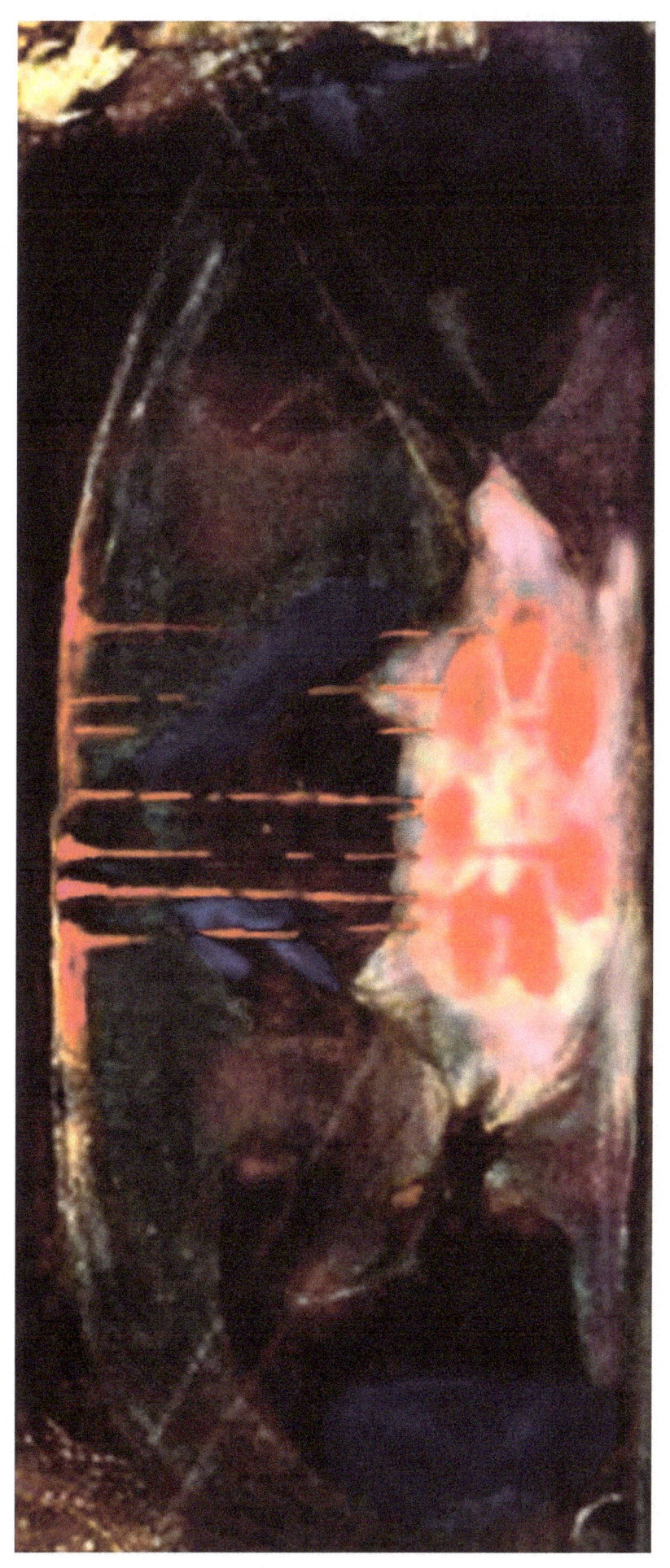

17 **The Subtereranean Figures** :  the Christ-force permeates the interior of the Earth.

wisdom, which has been preserved in the Icelandic text known as *The Edda*. In this scene there are also references to the Masonic legend of how, from the cross of Jesus, an acacia tree blossoms, a theme that we shall return to soon. If we view the entire Crucifixion scene together, then we have the figure of a tree; a kind of cosmic Tree of Life, the 'World-Tree' known as 'Yggdrasil' in the Edda. This tree here has its stem in the central area where the body of Jesus is placed, its roots are below the ground where the three dark entities are, and its foliage extends up above the body of Jesus. This idea of the cosmos as a great tree is also noted briefly in Egyptian Freemasonry, which notes that this image also occurs in the Rig Veda. In the Edda, underneath the Tree of Life are the three Norns, or feminine figures who represent the past, the present and the future; these three beings spin the threads of world karma. They are referred to in Old Icelandic literature as helping mothers in childbirth. But the reference by Anna May to 'Mothers' may be incorrect, as she perhaps means the mysterious spirit beings mentioned only very briefly by Rudolf Steiner. These beings are unlikely to be depicted here as Rudolf Steiner taught that they exist in the heights of Devachan.

So what then are these three beings, and why is this subterranean element depicted? They depict firstly the threefold soul forces, of thinking, feeling and willing, absorbing the divine spiritual energies or astral and Devachanic light which permeated the Earth at the death of Jesus. This process however, of gradually becoming a spiritual human being through the presence of the Christ-light in the soul and spirit, occurs more in the hidden recesses of the soul. It is as such not a process monitored by the "I" or ego, that is, by our normal consciousness. So it occurs down in the hidden depths of the human being. So the three beings from this viewpoint, represent our three soul qualities. However the Christ-light also permeates the remote depths of the planet's interior, down to its core.

Rudolf Steiner taught that the Earth's interior consists of a series of layers in spherical form (like that of an onion). In the centre of the Earth, below these eight layers, consisting of differing astral qualities, is its core. Some of these layers, especially number 5, the *Fructifying layer,* number 6, the *Fire-earth layer* and number 7, the *Reflector layer,* have potent malignant forces in them. The cosmic Christ's primary location within our planet's structure, is in its core; this is the realm of the Spirit of the Earth.[47] This means that the Christ light pervades the various layers of the Earth's interior, in order to enter the core of the planet's interior. So this planetary activity by the cosmic sun god, like the subtle influence of the Christ-light hidden in our normal consciousness, also occurs in a dark and hidden place.

As the human soul purifies itself and absorbs the spiritual light that helps to form the Spiritual-self, this same process has an impact upon the interior of the planet, illumining and purifying its various layers. About this process Rudolf Steiner revealed very little, but we can reasonably draw the conclusion that the three figures in the dark cave-like place also represent the spiritual beings that actually work with the developing spirituality in the human soul, interweaving this into the layers of the planet's interior. This is why they have a delicate bluish hue, alluding to the Spirit-self, and also why around them is a delicate reddish colouring, indicating the general presence of the Christ light in the Earth's interior, but also in the soul-forces of humanity, through permeating our blood-stream.

The next feature of this subterranean scene we need to contemplate is, that the Christ-force, represented as blood, being gathered up by the three beings, is forming into seven oval shapes. This is alluding to the rose-cross with its seven roses, although this symbol won't become formed until the Rosicrucian brotherhood is established in late medieval times. The entire painting is a holy revelation about esoteric Christianity, and a major part of this revelation focuses on the role of the leader of the Rosicrucian Movement. For this reason, the impact on humanity of the Christ-light, which now exists within our planet, is viewed from the perspective of the actions of the high initiate, Christian Rosencreutz.

It is helpful here to contemplate the profound knowledge of Rudolf Steiner about the karma of the holy initiate, Christian Rosencreutz; a karma which is unveiled in the painting. We learnt

---

[47] GA 97, lecture, 21st April, 1906.

earlier, that Hiram the master builder, living about 1,000 BC, had reincarnated as Lazaros, and had been initiated by Christ himself. It was this very close disciple of Christ, who was known as the "disciple who the Lord loved", and who wrote the Gospel of St. John. That is, this gospel was written by Lazaros, who after this initiation was called, Lazaros-John. That Lazaros-John would have a very lofty task in serving the Saviour is indicated in a striking passage at the end of the Gospel of St. John. When this passage is contemplated in the original Greek, it reveals a message that indicates the especial destiny of Lazaros-John and the arising of Rosicrucianism. In chapter 21, the Risen Jesus Christ appears to the disciples and has some questions for Peter. The dialogue somewhat poorly appears like this in most translations,

> Jn 21:15 When they had finished eating, Jesus said to Simon Peter, "Simon son of John, do you truly love me more than these?" "Yes, Lord," he said, "You know that I love you." Jesus said, "Feed my lambs."
> Jn 21:16 Again Jesus said, "Simon son of John, do you truly love me?" He answered, "Yes, Lord, you know that I love you." Jesus said, "Take care of my sheep."
> Jn 21:17 The third time he said to him, "Simon son of John, do you love me?" Peter was hurt because Jesus asked him the third time, "Do you love me?" He said, "Lord, you know all things; you know that I love you." Jesus said, "Feed my sheep".

In fact, the ancient Greek language had four verbs for what we today call "love". One of these is 'phileo' (φιλέω) which actually means just 'to like'; another verb is 'agapao' (ἀγαπάω), from which the noun 'agape' derives. This verb refers to a profound reality. It means to have 'good-will' in the profound sense of being inwardly in union with the core of the other person; we could think of this as a kind of 'will-unity'. Hence it usually refers to a love arising in the core of the soul, in its will-forces, rather than only in the emotions. It is a condition that requires a truly selfless, spiritual love, because the higher will of the human being is then active, and the higher will forces in humanity have a divine origin. In this dialogue, the Saviour has asked Peter if he has 'agape' (the profound, will-derived love) for Him, but Peter does not find it possible to affirm this. Instead he answers, "I like you"; so the dialogue is actually saying;

> Jn 21:15 When they had finished eating, Jesus said to Simon Peter, "Simon son of John, do you have within a **divine love** for me {*a higher-will unity* with me}, more than you have for these?" "Yes, Lord," he said, "You know that I **like** you." [48] Jesus said, "Feed my lambs."
> Jn 21:16 Again Jesus said, "Simon son of John, do you have within a **divine love** for me {*a higher-will unity*} with me?" He answered, "Yes, Lord, you know that I **like** you." Jesus said, "Take care of my sheep."
> Jn 21:17 The third time he said to him, "Simon son of John, do you **like** me?" Peter was hurt because Jesus asked him the third time, "Do you **like** me?" He said, "Lord, you know all things; you know that I **like** you." Jesus said, "Feed my sheep".

It is important here to note that the verb, 'agapao' is an exceptional verb, used for situations involving spiritual realities. It was also used in more human situations, but these often were about very high 'love', such as the love of a parent for a child, or the love that would lead a human being to sacrifice their life for another. It was used in the Hellenistic world specifically for a love between divine spirit beings, or from a divine being to a human being, usually an initiate or a king; both of these in reality require a profound will-unity to exist between the two beings in question. Since this love was a will-based dynamic, a vibrant living reality, the noun 'agape' from the verb 'agapao', appears to never have been used in Greek civilisation – until Jesus began to use it, to urge his disciples and followers to become people of this kind of love.[49] Then, Christians began to not only refer to 'loving', but also to this as a specific 'object', a specific reality: the noun, 'agape'.

---

[48] The core Greek text here is, λέγει αὐτῷ πάλιν δεύτερον, Σίμων Ἰωάννου, **ἀγαπᾷς** μὲ λέγει αὐτῷ, ναὶ κύριε, σὺ οἶδας ὅτι **φιλῶ** σε.

[49] As established in the article, "ἀγάπαω" in *Theologisches Wörterbuch zum Neuen Testament*, erster Bd, edit. G Kittel, Kohlhammer Vlg, Stuttgart, 1953.

So on the third occasion, the Saviour changes his admonishing query from 'agapao' to 'phileo', since Peter has shown that he cannot respond at the agape level. Now here we need to consider again that Lazaros-John is "the disciple whom the Lord loveth"; and of course in this phrase, the verb is 'agape'. So a difference between the two disciples is being indicated, but then comes a highly esoteric revelation about Lazaros-John;

> [Jn 21:20] Peter turned and saw that the disciple whom Jesus loved was following them. (This was the one who had leaned back against Jesus at the supper and had said, "Lord, who is going to betray you?")
> [Jn 21:21] When Peter saw him, he asked, "Lord, what about him?"
> [Jn 21:22] Jesus answered, "*If I will that he remains until I am appearing, what is that to you*? You, follow me." [50]

The expression, "until I am appearing" refers to what Rudolf Steiner explains as the re-appearing to humanity's consciousness of Christ (subtly in the ethers), an event which was destined to take place as of the 20th century; this is the so-called Second Coming of Christ. This remarkable reply hints at the extraordinary and blessed destiny about to unfold for Lazaros-John, as an initiate very close to Christ Jesus. He shall be gaining the eternal or 'deathless' consciousness of an adept (and the associated occult powers). His destiny will be focussed on the continual task of inspiring and strengthening Christian awareness in Christendom, to help prepare people to be receptive to the influences from Christ when He re-appears. In the course of this mission, Lazaros-John will eventually become the founder of the Rosicrucian movement. In the subterranean scene of the painting, the seven blood-red oval shapes are pointing ahead to the sacred mission of Christian Rosencreutz, he who appears in the right-side column underneath 'Hellas'. That is, this great initiate will be establishing the Rosicrucian movement, which will have the rose-cross as its primary sacred symbol.

He would also be bringing about important spiritual impulses in the cultural life. Rudolf Steiner implies for example, his influence with Leonardo da Vinci (*the Last Supper*).[51] Rudolf Steiner reveals that Lazaros-John has been incarnate in every century since the time of Christ, although 'an incarnation' in this case need not always mean being physically born, but rather overshadowing a person.

### Joseph of Arimathea

Anna May identified the person shown kneeling at the foot of the cross, and holding a cup in which to receive some of the holy blood, as Joseph of Arimathea. Here he is the only physical witness to the crucifixion scene depicted in the painting, although we know that other people were there. The Gospels reveal that he was a member of the Jewish ruling council, the Sanhedrin, and a wealthy follower of Jesus who requested the body of Jesus from Pontius Pilate, in order to give it proper burial. The episode painted here, of collecting some blood of Jesus, is not found in the Gospels; it derives from a poem about the Holy Grail, written between the late 12th to early 13th centuries, by a French poet, Robert de Boron. The legendary material found in the various Grail cycles derives from esoteric wisdom, which the Grail writers were inspired to write, or to recount as troubadours from village to village. In showing the collecting of the sacred blood in a cup, Rudolf Steiner is affirming the deep spiritual truths contained in such legends.

Before we look further at the Grail motif, we need to note some unusual features of this scene, Firstly, the colour and shape of the clothing worn by St. Joseph is what we normally associate with the Virgin Mary. The outer garment is the traditional deep blue colour of her cloak; and the head-scarf, with its bluish tinge, has a feminine quality. But Anna May states that, it is Joseph of Arimathea; so how do we understand his clothing? He was a member of the Sanhedrin, the Priestly ruling council, and it is known that high priests in ancient Israel wore a blue coloured, sleeveless robe over a white tunic. This does match, to some extent, what the person is wearing in the painting. But Hebrew priests also wore a cone-shaped turban, whereas the person here has

---

[50] The Greek here is:... ἐὰν αὐτὸν θέλω μένειν ἕως ἔρχομαι, τί πρὸς σέ σύ μοι ἀκολούθει.
[51] We can also surmise that his influence lies behind Matthias Grunewald's world masterpiece, *the Isenheim Altarpiece,* and in the writings of Shakespeare.

a flat head-covering which appears somewhat feminine. After we have considered the Grail motif here, we shall return to this unusual feature. Before we contemplate the nature of the Holy Grail, we need to note that the actual grail cup or chalice held by Joseph is not really visible, as it surrounded by a radiance that obscures it. But, very significantly, below the chalice, there is an unusual rounded patch of blue; this patch of blue and the feminine clothing are both linked to a profound aspect of cosmic Christianity. We shall return to these strange features, later (p. 56).

**The Holy Grail**
The medieval Holy Grail legends present several different definitions of this especially sacred theme. The Grail can be an actual cup, or an emerald stone, or the physical blood of Jesus (a small amount of this), a mysterious chalice, and also a kind of nourishment.[52] Our painting includes the feature of Joseph of Arimathea gathering up some of the blood of Jesus, but why? What aspect of the Holy Grail is being indicated here?

**The Two Columns within the human being**
In addition, when contemplating this painting, one also has to bear in mind that the astral qualities of a person permeate their bloodstream (and also to some extent, their etheric energies). The two columns here, with their red tones, framing the depiction of the Christ-event, also represent the blood-stream of the human being, and thus humanity's soul qualities. These two columns allude to the two columns in Freemason lodges, and these also have some resonance with an esoteric theme presented by Rudolf Steiner in his lectures on the Apocalyptic 'seals' displayed in 1907 at the major Munich conference.[53] In his lectures on these images he comments in regard to the fourth seal, which has two columns: one is red, the other is a mixture of red and blue. He taught that, when, in Lemurian times, human beings began to breathe in air, and the Mars forces permeated the Earth with iron, the blood stream began to be red and to be permeated by oxygen. Then, he explained, if you imagine this bloodstream as a separate system within the human being standing upright before you, the red blood can be viewed, in terms of esoteric Biblical imagery, as **the Tree of Knowledge of Good and Evil, meaning the earthly ego-sense.**

But also in us there is the other tree, a blue-red tree, meaning our bloodstream permeated by carbon, and this can be viewed as **the Tree of Death.** As Rudolf Steiner explains, it had been the Tree of Life, but was transformed into the Tree of Death, for what had been red blood (carrying the fresh oxygen) is now blue, or blue-red, with old blood, with its carbon dioxide. This is a physiological way of viewing the story of the Fall of Man. Blue blood is the physical expression of what happens to the Tree Of Knowledge, because, apart from the carbon dioxide, body cells are killed with every thought, with every use of the mind, and having now the dead carbon cells in it, it becomes the Tree Of Death. But in the future, as the Higher-self is developed, the human being will be able to transform the Tree of Death into a Tree of Life. This esoteric perspective refers to the future wherein the human being develops a true Tree of Life and a true Tree of Knowledge, becoming a cosmic being, no longer having decaying ethers and being subject to disease. In this painting, the blood of the Saviour is placed between these two, both as a reality and as a symbol, suggesting that the process of humanity evolving from the Tree of Death to the Tree of Life, is being made possible by the deed of Christ.

The chalice which Joseph of Arimathea is holding, is placed artistically within the sacred bloodstream from above, from the wounds of the Saviour; whilst below Joseph is the symbolic bloodstream inside the Earth, and hence also, as we noted above, in the subconscious part of the soul of human beings. Here we shall consider a selection of lecture extracts from Rudolf Steiner which are especially helpful in the quest to understand the significance of the Holy Grail in this painting. One explanation from Rudolf Steiner as to what the Grail is, reveals that the Grail Mysteries were part of the Rosicrucian movement, and therefore of its modern form, anthroposophy,

---

[52] There are also irrelevant, blasphemous misinterpretations of the Grail, involving Mary Magdalene, see my *Rudolf Steiner Handbook* for brief indications about this.
[53] These lectures are published in German in GA 284-5.

> The pupil {of the medieval Rosicrucian movement} had to educate himself to perceive in every single flower in the meadows that he crosses, the external expression of a living being; the expression of the spirit dwelling in the earth....everything transient becomes a signifier of an eternal reality, which expresses itself through such a transient object. Feelings of this kind had to be attained by pupils of the Rosicrucians and by the disciples of the Grail. The teacher would say, "Behold the flower chalice which receives the ray of the sun. The sun calls forth the pure reproductive forces which slumber in the plant, and hence the sun's rays were called the 'holy lance of love'".[54]

The above words provide a valuable introduction to this theme, and at the same time, they also hint at its deepest meaning. The next lecture extract provides some vital orientation towards understanding the esoteric truths enshrined in our painting, about the link between Christian Rosencreutz and the Grail,

> Those who {in medieval times} called themselves 'Johannine' Christians, whose symbol was the Rose-Cross, understood {as regards the proclamation of the re-birth of humanity through the Mystery of Golgotha}, that precisely what was reborn for mankind as the secret of its higher ego **has been preserved** – preserved by the close community which grew out of Rosicrucianism. This element which offers rebirth, is symbolized by the sacred vessel from which Christ Jesus ate and drank with his disciples, and in which Joseph of Arimathea caught the blood that flowed from the wound: the Holy Grail, which as the legend recounts, was brought by Angels to Europe. The legends recount that a temple was built in which to place this vessel, and the Rosicrucians became the guardians of what it contained; the essence of the reborn divinity.

> The mystery of the reborn god had its being in humanity. It is the mystery of the Grail, a Mystery put forward as a new gospel, proclaiming: We look up to a sage such as the writer of the Gospel of St. John, who was able to say, "In the beginning was the Word, and the Word was with God, and a God was the Word. That which was 'with God' in the beginning was born again in Him whom we have seen suffer and die on Golgotha, and who is risen again." This continuity throughout all time of the divine principle and its rebirth; this is what the author of St. John's Gospel intended to present. Something known to all those who endeavoured to proclaim this truth was that, what had existed in the beginning, had been preserved.

> In the beginning there existed the mystery of the higher ego; it is {now} preserved in the Grail; it has remained linked to the Grail. And in the Grail there lives the ego united with the Eternal and Immortal, just as the lower ego is linked to what is transient and mortal. The person who knows the secret of the Holy Grail, knows that from the wood of the Cross there springs forth ever new life: the immortal ego, which is symbolized by the roses on the black wood of the cross.[55]

The term, "Johannine Christians" as used by Rudolf Steiner, refers to those followers of Christ who develop an especially close connection to the Gospel of St. John, and the esoteric and cosmic perspectives about the Christ-impulse, taught in anthroposophical Rosicrucianism. This kind of Christianity is distinct from the theology developed in the normal churches, especially the church of Rome, which could be referred to as "Petrine" theology, meaning a non-esoteric theology, associated with St. Peter, since he was an early bishop in Rome, the city from which western Christianity would develop as a non-esoteric religion. The next lecture extract presents a wonderful contemplative approach to understanding the Holy Grail,

> In the temple of the human body is located a Holy of Holies. Many people live in the temple without knowing about it. But those who sense it, receive from it the power to purify themselves so that they may enter into this sacred place. There is the sacred vessel which was prepared through epochs of time. There rests the holy Chalice which

---

[54] GA 99, lecture 6th June, 1907.
[55] GA 112, lecture, 24th June, 1909.

was prepared through epochs of time so that it would be ready when the time came to hold the blood of Christ, {that is} the life of Christ. When the human being has entered this place he has also found the path to the Holy of Holies in the great Earth temple.

Many on Earth live there too, without knowing it; but if the human being has found himself in his innermost sanctuary, he will also be allowed to enter the great Earth temple and find the Holy Grail. Firstly the chalice will appear to him, carved as though from wonderful gleaming crystal that form symbols and letters; then gradually he will sense its holy content, so that the content itself shines for him in a golden radiance. A human being then enters into the Mystery place of his own heart, and then a divine being emerges from this {human} mystery centre and connects itself to the God without, with the Christ being. This divine being lives in the spiritual light which streams into the chalice, hallowing it.[56]

We shall consider the implication of these sacred truths, later in the book. The final lecture extract presents the essence of what the cosmic nature of Christianity is, and also teaches that the achievement of finding the Grail within oneself, is a process which was made possible by the Mystery of Golgotha,

With the event on Golgotha, as the blood flowed from the wounds of the great Redeemer, as the Cosmic Heart's blood permeated the Earth, right into the core of the planet, the Earth started to glow; from deep within, light began to stream out, into the surrounds. Through this, the possibility was also given for each human individual to experience itself in this light. As the Earth became the body of the great sun-spirit, in that He permeated the planet with his spiritual forces, then all life on the planet was also given these forces. The physical body of Jesus of Nazareth was the mediator through which the forces for the cosmos streamed out at Golgotha...the human being can experience this light in itself as an earthly human being, as he or she recognizes himself or herself as a part of the Earth which is now the body of the cosmic Christ.[57]

It is the above aspects of the Holy Grail that are the most important, and which are of relevance to the painting; the theme of an actual physical cup, and where it may be now, is not as important. There is implicit in all these words from Rudolf Steiner, that it is through seeking high spirituality, whilst here in earthly life, that the Grail – the outcome of the sacrifice on Golgotha – can be attained. This same perspective is to be found in the magnificent Grail saga of Wolfram von Eschenbach written in medieval German. In Book Five, paragraph 235, he describes how the Grail is carried by the Grail Queen, called "the Repose of Joy", who carries it on a special fine green cloth...

She carried the perfection of Paradise: both root and branch.
It was a thing, called the Grail: the all-surpassing earthly blessing.

( Truoc sie den Wunsch von Paradis, bede wurzeln und ris.
Daz war ein dinc, das hiez der Gral, erden wunschen uberwal.)

A glimpse into the divine spiritual power of the Grail, is given in the words of Rudolf Steiner when the Anthroposophical Society was founded in 1913. He reveals how its spiritual energies, once they are present in the human being, can rejuvenate what has been deadened by the lower self – that is, the influences of Lucifer and Ahriman,

The Holy Grail is surrounded by many, many, mysteries.... in the Holy Grail {knowledge of earlier centuries} if understood in its true nature, there was embraced everything which characterised the secrets of the human soul in {our} later times....The Holy Grail was, and is, nothing else than That which can so nurture the living part of the soul that it can become master of the dead part {of the soul}. Montsalvat, the sanctuary of the Holy

---

[56] GA 265 p. 418.

[57] GA 265 p. 418.

Grail is the school in which one has to learn, for the sake of the still living part of the soul...what has to be poured into the still living part of the soul in order for it become master of the part of the physical body that has 'died', and that part of the soul which has become unconscious.[58]

These words indicate why the Grail, on a spiritual level, is also described as a living nourishment for the soul. We shall return to this theme later, when we contemplate the figure of St. Paul.

**Initiatory secrets: Joseph of Arimathea or the Earth-soul ?**
We noted above, Joseph of Arimathea is dressed in a somewhat feminine garment, and also there is a strange, rounded patch of blue underneath the chalice held by St. Joseph; these two features are included to allow a deep truth about the Mystery of Golgotha to be conveyed. This truth is not about the person of Jesus the man, but a greater, non-human being. We also noted earlier that to initiatory consciousness, in St. John's Gospel, chapter 13, verse 18, the colossal truth is being conveyed that there exists a cosmic Christ, in addition to Jesus, and that this deity is soon to become the indwelling spirit of the Earth. A truth which has been kept veiled, only subtly indicated in early Christian texts. But Rudolf Steiner, through the inspiration from the Christ-Impulse, specifically spoke of this to his students, making this a core truth of anthroposophical understanding of Christianity. So, here the painting is telling us that not only did Joseph of Arimathea gather some of the holy blood into a chalice, but also the Earth-soul itself (or herself) became a chalice for the divine light and Life-spirit of the great sun god, the solar logos.

In doing this Rudolf Steiner has directly echoed in artistic form a secret initiatory teaching, hidden within St. John's Gospel, which like the sentence in 13:18 proclaims the reality of the cosmic aspect to Christ. The sentence in this Gospel, which we recall, was written by he who later became Christian Rosencreutz, speaks of the permeating of the Earth's soul by the great Sun-god. The passage which this scene is directly referring to, is John, 19:23:

> When the soldiers crucified Jesus, they took his clothes, dividing them into four shares, one for each of them, with the undergarment remaining. This garment was seamless, woven in one piece from top to bottom.

Translated much more accurately, using the new text assessment method which this author is developing, the Initiatory Critical Analysis approach, it reads as follows:

> When the soldiers crucified Jesus, they took his cloaks {four-sectioned cloak}, dividing this into four segments, one for each of them, and {also} his fine tunic. In fact, this tunic was woven as a seamless garment, from the top downwards. Therefore......

We can conclude, from various statements of Rudolf Steiner, that when Lazaros-John wrote his Gospel it was a process in which was interwoven inspiration of the Saviour himself. In particular Rudolf Steiner described the gospel writers as writing from "a Resurrection memory", meaning that the Saviour was assisting their recollection of what the three years have really meant. This understanding of how the Gospels were written, is echoed in the writings of a very early Christian thinker, Justin Martyr, "...the apostles in their memoirs, called "Gospels" delivered to us {Christians} that which they were required to do..."[59] Through this process, and using the Greek language, deep, deep truths of the Christ-Reality were embedded within Scripture. The above sentence – astonishing as it is, when correctly translated – opens a portal to sacred truths of cosmic Christianity.

The Greek text states that Jesus is wearing a "fine tunic", meaning a woman's tunic, or 'a tunic worn by the High Priest' and that his cloak is plural; i.e., cloaks. Why ? Naturally, scholars choose the second meaning, that of the 'tunic of the High Priest', concluding that Jesus deliberately put on such a strictly forbidden garment (worn only by the High Priest), or that the evangelist deliberately described him as wearing this, for theological reasons. But to translate the word as 'woman's tunic' is more correct, because firstly, if Jesus had been wearing the High Priest's tunic,

---

[58] GA 144, lecture 7th Feb. 1913.
[59] The Writings of Justin Martyr, ca. AD 140, in First Apology", section 66.

this would have been discovered at his trial and very much emphasized as evidence of political intention to undermine the worldly authority of the Sanhedrin – which he never had. Secondly, his outer garment(s), the cloak, is not a garment ever worn by Hebrew priests, so his clothing over-all would then be inconsistent.[60]

For Jesus' inner clothing to be described as a very fine, seamless, woman's garment, points to the intention in this sentence here, to move from a focus on Jesus and his clothing, to a focus on the mother Earth and the cosmic Christ. As Rudolf Steiner explained, what is meant by a 'seamless woman's tunic' is actually the seamless, unified atmosphere and ether-body of the Earth-soul, (thought of as feminine): the atmosphere, the all-enveloping firmament with its ethers, which surrounds our planet. That this is actually the meaning here (and not tunic 'of the High Priest') is demonstrated by the astonishing fact that in addition, Jesus' **cloak** is actually called "**cloaks**" in Greek – which is an impossibility – but it becomes clear that it is a cloak which is fourfold in its structure.[61] There are said to be four soldiers who are at the cross. This fourfold 'cloak' refers to the fourfold Earth. That is, the Earth with its fourfold qualities. These qualities include the main landmasses, the four ether layers (the life-ether, light-ether, tone-ether and warmth-ether), its four realms of living creatures (mineral, plant, animal, human), and so on. As Rudolf Steiner explained about this sentence, "the tunic is the undividable atmosphere of the Earth....the cloak which is divided into four parts, represents the four main landmasses {of the planet}.[62]

In other words, the Gospel here, whilst referring to the physical garments on the body of the man Jesus now going to other people, is also subtly pointing to the reverse dynamic happening on a cosmic scale: mother Earth, now, at the death of Jesus, receiving the cosmic Christ into its atmosphere: its etheric and astral aura, and its fourfold nature. That this is the secret initiatory meaning is confirmed by another discreet use of Greek grammar. The next sentence in the Gospel, after empathizing that the tunic was seamless is, in the NIV Bible,

> Therefore the soldiers said, "let us not tear it, but cast lots for it, to see whose it shall be".

But the verb used here is translated incorrectly by convention in our Bibles; for it is actually saying,

> Therefore the soldiers said, "May Divine Will determine, regarding this garment, whose it shall be".[63]

This correct translation, points the reader to the intention of higher Powers in regard to the Earth's soul, and thus, to the intense confusion of conventional non-esoteric theology, steps quite openly out of the historical narrative, and into the esoteric-cosmic meaning: namely that the Divine Will has the intention that the great Sun-god shall take possession of the Earth. So it seems that these are the reasons for the pale blue round-ish shape being placed near to the chalice held by St. Joseph.[64]

---

[60] The Old Testament in Greek (the Septuagint) in describing, in Exodus, the priest's clothing, does not use this word for the garments.
[61] The word for 'cloaks' can also mean 'various garments', but not here, as the other garment, the tunic, is separately mentioned.
[62] GA 94, lecture 6th Nov. 1906.
[63] The verb (lagchano λαγχάνω ) always means A: 'to receive by divine will'; or B: for deities to cast the lot for humans. .
[64] My *The Hellenistic Mysteries and Christianity* explores some Biblical texts in relation to Christ as the Earth-spirit.

18 The Upper part of the Tree of Life: a pentagram, an ouroboros serpent, an alchemical matrass.

**The Middle Section, above:**

Before we contemplate the features in the upper part of the middle section of the great triptych painting, we need to note that it concerns the achievement of spirituality, the redemption and renewal of the human being. In anthroposophical understanding, the human spirit is a divine or 'Devachanic' reality, whereas our soul is an 'astral' reality. Similar to our soul, our spirit is also perceived by the seer as an auric glow, but consisting of much higher 'energies' than our soul. The human spirit is threefold, just as we have three aspects to our soul.

The human spirit consists of the Spirit-self or spiritualized soul qualities, also called 'Manas' in theosophical terms; the Life-spirit or spiritualized life-energies (etheric body) or 'Buddhi', and the Spirit-human or spiritualized will-forces that underlie the physical body. The spirit-human is the 'Atman' in theosophical terms. Rudolf Steiner used the theosophical terms at times, especially in the first decade of his teaching.

**The legend of the Cross**
As we noted earlier, in this upper area are features that have arisen from the cross; they have 'grown out of it'. Firstly, we see that the wood of the cross has become a tree, in the branches of which are some very interesting esoteric images, see illustration 18. This profound motif, of a tree springing from the Cross on Golgotha, formed part of the Rosicrucian esoteric teachings. In this, a cutting from the original Tree of Life, planted on Adam's grave, is linked to the Temple of Solomon, and via the Queen of Sheba, to the Cross on Golgotha. Rudolf Steiner described this legend as it exists in Freemason texts, and then commented on it to his theosophical Freemasonry students,

> The Christian legend about the Cross is as follows. We shall begin with it:
>
> " The wood or tree from which the Cross had been taken is not simply wood, but – so the legend relates – it was, originally an offshoot of the Tree of Life, which had been cut for Adam, the first human. This offshoot was planted in the earth by Adam's son, Seth, and the young tree developed three trunks which grew intertwined. Later Moses cut the famous staff from this wood. Then, in the legend, the same wood plays a role in connection with King Solomon's Temple in Jerusalem. That is, it was to have been used as a main pillar, in building the Temple. But then something peculiar came to light. It could not be used in the Temple, so it was laid across a brook, as a bridge.
>
> Here it was little valued until the Queen of Sheba came; as she was crossing it, she saw just what this piece of wood really was. She had for the first time re-discovered the significance of the wood {used for this} bridge, which was there between the two realms, for crossing over the stream – from the bank on this side over to the bank on the other side. So then it happened that the Cross on which the Redeemer hung was made out of this {same} wood, after which it was taken on its various further travels. "
>
> Thus you see that the point of this legend has to do with the origin and evolution of the human race. Adam's son, Seth, is supposed to have taken this offspring from the Tree of Life, which grew three trunks. These three trunks symbolise the three principles, the three eternal forces of nature, Manas, Buddhi and Atma, which have grown together and form the trinity which is the foundation of all growth and all development. It is apt that Seth – the son of Adam who took the place of Abel, murdered by Cain – should have planted the offspring of the original Tree in the earth.
>
> You know that on the one hand we are dealing with the Cain current {of evolution} and on the other hand with the descendants of Abel and Seth. The sons of Cain, who work upon the outer world, cultivate the sciences and arts in particular. They are the ones who bring in the stones from the outer world to build the Temple. It is through their art that the Temple is to be built. The descendants of the line of Abel/Seth are the so-called Sons of

God, who cultivate the true spiritual part of man's nature. These two currents were always somewhat in antithesis. On the one hand we have the worldly activity of man, the development of those sciences which serve man's comfort and outward life in general; on the other hand we have the Sons of God, occupied with the development of man's higher attributes. We must make ourselves clear about it: the viewpoint from which the Legend of the True Cross springs, makes a firm distinction between the mere outward building of the World Temple through science and technology, and what, as something deeply imbued with religious piety, is active towards the sanctification of the whole Temple of Humanity.

Only because this Temple of Humanity is given a higher task - only because the outer building, so to speak, serving as it does only a mere usefulness, makes itself into an expression of the House of God - can it become a receptacle for the spiritual, Inner-part in which the higher tasks of humanity are nurtured. Only because *Strength* for striving towards divine virtue, {gives} external form to *Beauty*, so that the Word - which serves the external activities of people - is thereby placed in the service of divine *Wisdom*, does this *Strength* attain its fulfilment. For thereby is the Worldly transformed into the Godly. When the three virtues, *Wisdom*, *Beauty* and *Strength*, become the receptacle of the divine, then shall the Temple of Humanity be perfected. This is the perspective underlying the worldview that is underlying this legend. [65]

## A new Tree of Life

Here in the painting by Anna May, this profoundly esoteric Rosicrucian legend is specifically depicted. In anticipation of the Resurrection, the Cross has already blossomed into a new Tree of Life, in which three remarkable esoteric symbols are placed.[66] But firstly, we note how the leaves on the left side of the tree are sparse and dark, indicating that the divine light has faded from the Earth, so the world was in dire need of a renewal. The first symbol that we see in the tree is a round object, in which is inscribed a pentagram shape with its own circumference traced out around it. A pentagram contained within a round shape is sometimes referred to as a pentacle, and as such has become very widespread in New Age mystical and occult circles; these various groups interpret this form in various ways. The pentagram is found in Freemasonry, where it is explained in general mystical terms, that aren't relevant to our painting.

## The Pentagram

In anthroposophy, the pentagram has two meanings. Primarily, it is explained as a symbol of the Holy Spirit, and this aspect is presented in lectures where Rudolf Steiner also proceeds to explain the hexagram as a symbol of the Logos and hence, in regard to humanity, of the Life-spirit (or Buddhi). So we then can conclude that the pentagram, as a symbol of the Holy Spirit, is also a symbol with regard to human beings, of the Spiritual-self.[67] Secondly, the pentagram depicts actual currents in the etheric body of the human being. But it is the former meaning which is relevant to the painting. The pentagram in the tree is indicating that, as a result of the events of Golgotha, the Earth's aura is now permeated by the divine light of the cosmic Christ, and this enables individual human beings to attain their Spiritual-self.

That the pentagram here has an enclosure around it, and is within an oval, presents the Spiritual-self as a definite, definable entity. We can also note here, that the orbit of Venus around the Earth, viewed in a geo-centric way, as it repeatedly traces out its path over some years, forms a pentagram shape (this fact was known in ancient Sumerian times, about 3,000 BC). When the Spiritual-self is formed, then the higher astral energies from Venus are present in the person's aura; so this also is a factor linking the pentagram to the Spiritual-self.

---

[65] GA 93, lecture, 29th May, 1905.
[66] This has a similarity to the Crucifixion scene in the sublime, Rosicrucian-inspired painting by Matthias Grunewald (1505); there the cross on which the Saviour hangs, is bent slightly downwards, as if anticipating the mighty upwards surge of the resurrected Jesus Christ.
[67] GA 94, lecture, 9th June, 1906.

### The Ouroboros

Just above the pentagram, and indeed partially in its space, is the next symbol: a serpent with its tail in its mouth. This symbol, known in ancient Greek times as an Ouroboros, represents the next spiritual achievement for the human being: Buddhi or the Life-Spirit. It is also used as a symbol in the Egyptian Freemasonry rites, on various vestments. When this high stage is achieved, then the meditant's consciousness reaches beyond time, and enters into the Devachanic realms, where eternality or non-time conditions exist. It brings such high consciousness that all of one's previous incarnations are known and integrated into the sense of "I", which becomes thereby transformed into an eternal "I". Rudolf Steiner described the Ouroboros condition as meaning that, "...the I is {now} extending beyond the earthly sphere."[68] Rudolf Steiner once described this mysterious spiritual part of us from the viewpoint of the etheric forces in this way,

> Visualize the usual life-forces now conserved by a pure, restrained harmonious life-style, and then made to resonate, to respond, to the utterly outpouring, selfless compassion of the Spirit-self. [69]

The etheric body in effect becomes divine as the Life-Spirit develops; and as this process gets underway, healing powers and artistic skills arise. The condition of a divinely enhanced etheric body is especially closely linked to the Cosmic Christ, from whose own divine cosmic Life-Spirit, the Earth and human beings receive their Life-spirit, as the etheric body transforms. This is one of the esoteric truths behind the words of Christ in the gospels, "I am the bread of life." As we noted above, the Ouroboros serpent is partially intersecting the pentagram. The reason for this is, that the Life-spirit condition gradually develops once the Spirit-self has been attained; there is a transitional phase before it is fully developed.

### The Son of Man

When Christ Jesus refers to the "the Son of Man", he is using a Mystery term for a person who has attained the Spirit-self and is beginning to develop their Life-spirit.[70] It is also obvious that this term is used by Christ Jesus to refer to himself, in that he is the archetype of the future redeemed human being; so some of his references to the Son of Man are ambiguous, in a deliberate sense. For example in the Gospel of St. John, *"Just as Moses lifted up the snake in the desert, so the Son of Man must be lifted up"* (3:14). This sentence does make some reference to the lifting up of Jesus onto a cross at Golgotha, but its main reference is to the developing of the astral and etheric bodies, up to the level of the Spirit-self, with some presence of the Life-spirit.

But there is another sentence in St. John's Gospel (8:28) which also interweaves two meanings, and which is very relevant to this scene.[71] The sentence which is relevant here to the painting, occurs in St. John's Gospel 8:28,

> Jn 8:28 So Jesus said, "When you have lifted up the Son of Man, then you will know that I am the one I claim to be and that I do nothing on my own but speak these things which the Father has taught me.
> Jn 8:29 The one who sent me is with me; he has not left me alone, for I always do what pleases him."

But there is a much deeper meaning interwoven into the Greek text of the Gospels here; a level which is disclosed when the New Testament is approached on the initiatory level, as I explained in *The Hellenistic Mysteries and Christianity*. On the normal level, and using the understanding of the text as presented in the usual translations, this sentence is about the soon to occur death, by crucifixion, of Jesus, as the 'Son of Man'. It also emphasizes the close inner presence of the

---

[68] In GA 266a p. 405.
[69] GA 54, lecture 15th Feb. 1906, p. 289.
[70] GA 94, p. 291.
[71] At an Australian College of Divinity, this author has pioneered a new pathway to engaging with the text, intended to uncover initiatory meanings hidden within the text.

Father-God within Jesus. Whilst this meaning is entirely true, there is an even deeper meaning hidden here. On an initiatory level, the veiled meaning refers to the 'Son of Man' as the individual person seeking initiatory consciousness: this meaning provides profound insights into the message of the central part of our painting. The ancient Greek text can also be accurately translated as this:

> *So Jesus said, Whensoever you have **exalted** the Son of Man, then you will know that **I am the I am** {in you}; also {you will know in yourself} "I do nothing from myself, but only as the Father taught me".* These things I speak and moreover the One having sent me, is with me. He has not left me alone, for I always do that which is pleasing to Him.

The first sentence has the complex, veiled grammar in it, because it is referring to profound secrets of initiation, whilst the second sentence, "*These things I speak and also...*" is straightforward, and refers to Jesus' historical situation, as he addresses a crowd.

The first sentence is about the achieving of the Spirit-self, as a result of the deeds on Golgotha, and this is a central theme in the painting. At the stage of initiation where the Son of Man is exalted, the person becomes aware that their "I" – now becoming eternal – derives from the cosmic Christ. It is understood in anthroposophy, that the Spirit-self (an aspect of the higher "I") derives from the Holy Spirit, which through the deed of Christ of Golgotha has been brought within reach of seeking human souls. Whereas the Life-Spirit (another aspect of the higher "I") actually comes from the cosmic Christ, and now permeates the Earth's aura.

But moreover, with this second sentence, the Father-god, from whom the Atma or Spirit-human derives, is brought into a relationship to the higher "I". A person who achieves the Life-spirit, starts to become subtly aware of the Atma, the divine will energies of the Spirit-human, since the Spirit-human starts to develop at this stage. An alchemical feature in the painting points to the Atma or Spirit-human.

**Alchemy: an overview**
In our painting, just above the symbol for the Life-spirit, is placed a symbol for the Atma or Spirit-human: an object is known in alchemy as a Matrass or Phiol. Above the Ouroboros serpent is a tall, narrow-necked object, containing a substance. In the language of alchemy, it is in this flask-like matrass that a special substance, described as either a powder or a fluid (called a tincture) was placed, which, when subject to a heating process, conjured forth the so-called **Philosopher's stone.**

Since an alchemical symbol occurs in this painting, we need to have an overview of this subject, from an anthroposophical viewpoint, so far as that is possible from the brief indications Rudolf Steiner gave. He refers to the three well-known aspects of alchemy: a materialistic side, a medicinal-healing aspect, and a purely spiritual quest, also described in alchemical terms. In the materialistic aspect, alchemists attempted to produce gold from base metals, a process which exercised a magical spell over the minds of those doing this. They were affected by the possibility of achieving occult powers that this activity relied upon, as well as the wealth that it would bestow, if successful.

With regard to this side of alchemy, it is interesting to note that as alchemy gradually gave way to chemistry in the Age of Enlightenment, the efforts by such alchemists to achieve the physical transmutation of base metals via a retort and a matrass, etc., was echoed by the processes developed by the pioneers of industrial chemistry. One report of these early chemistry experiments, from 1829, involved an attempt to produce diamonds. The process has some similarities to the reports of the materialistically oriented medieval alchemists who sought to transmute base metals into gold,

> ...some carburet of sulphur, a transparent colourless liquid...is heated to redness in a porcelain tube {*this was called an Athanor in medieval times*}...several rolls of phosphorous were then introduced and covered with water...the phosphorous dissolves

and, becoming liquid, is poured into a matrass. The whole mass then divides {*in the matrass*} into three distinct layers: the first formed of pure water, the second is of carburet of sulphur, the third is liquid phosphorous...if the matrass is then agitated, the liquor grows thick, becomes milky and...separates anew into two layers...between these layers is a very thin stratum of fine white powder, which, when the matrass is exposed to the sun's rays, exhibits all the colours of the rainbow, which a little later became small crystals.....

The report goes on to state that these crystals were examined by "an experienced Paris jeweller" who pronounced them to be authentic diamonds.[72](!) This report, just before the dawn of 20th century science, takes us back into precisely the intriguing, enchanting quality of medieval materialistic alchemy. Just how a modern journal today, of good repute, would handle such a report – to all appearances, serious and meaning to be scientific – is an interesting question.

The second aspect, the therapeutic aspect of alchemy, has to do with research undertaken by medieval physicians, in an attempt to access etheric forces for the good of others; that is, to enhance the healing capacity of various elixirs and other medicines. This approach to alchemy is embodied in the words of Paracelsus, "Many have said about alchemy that it makes silver and gold. However such an attitude is indeed not to be taken up, but alone those special preparations are to be dealt with, which may become virtue and power in medicaments."[73] Rudolf Steiner explained that the ancient versions of medieval alchemy involved specific clairvoyant-occult powers which rested in the alchemist interacting with a variety of spirit beings.[74]

In regard to the third aspect of alchemy, the quest for higher consciousness, the complex language of alchemy was used to refer to spiritual development processes, undertaken by Rosicrucians, through various soul exercises. Rudolf Steiner told one audience, the "alchemy represented to the true Rosicrucians is nothing other than a symbol of the purification of the soul, the development of specific human virtues."[75] The Rosicrucian alchemical spiritual quest is viewed in the context of the Christ-reality; the matrass shown here in the painting refers to this third aspect of alchemical strivings. But there is another aspect to the approach of the Rosicrucians to alchemy, and this concerns a transitional reality, where matter and the ethers meet. This reality is also the realm that the materialistic, and the medical-herbalist, alchemists were seeking to access for their respective purposes. As Rudolf Steiner taught,

> There exists {in creation} a certain transitional reality, between the coarser matter and the finer. We can direct our attention to the boundary between the ethers and physical matter. What exists there, between physical and etheric reality is not similar to anything in our world. What is there, is neither gold, silver, lead or copper. There we have something which cannot be compared to any physical substance, but is the essence of them all. We have there a substance in which all other physical substances are contained; thus the other physical substances can be regarded as a modification of this one 'substance'.[76]

Before we consider further words from Rudolf Steiner about alchemy, let's consider a rare and important legend which links these themes. It existed one and a half thousand years ago in eastern Christian cultures, but has been forgotten to western Christianity for many centuries. It indicates the connection of the cosmic Christ forces to the finding of the Philosopher's Stone (or Stone of the Sages). The concept of the Philosopher's Stone and hence the term "Stone of the Sages", has been in use at least since the AD 300, when it is mentioned by Zosimus, a renowned alchemical writer. Zosimus himself was a member of, or was influenced by, the Manichaeans.

---

[72] *Virginia Literary Museum, Journal of Belle-Lettres, arts, etc, No. 1 Vol. 1* June 17 1829.

[73] Quoted in, *Die Spagyrische Kunst*, by Albert Hofmann, p. 10, 1923, Joh. Baum Vlg, Pfullingen.
[74] GA 232, p.199.
[75] GA 55, p.175.
[76] GA 130, lecture p. 65.

This Legend of the Sages' Stone was found in central Asia in about 1900, written in the ancient Uiguric language, and survives in a fragmentary form. It is dated to the seventh century AD, and will have been introduced to the Uighur people by priests or priestesses representing the Manichaeans, who had knowledge of high initiatory Christian wisdom. It was still known in the Orient in the thirteenth century, for Marco Polo encountered this same legend during his journeys into the Far East. The origin of this legend lies with the Manichaeans, as this text was discovered in 1904 in an ancient Manichaean document written about 500 AD. It serves as a meditation on the connection of Christ to the Philosophers' Stone. I translate this legend from the German translation of the original 'Sogdian' text, by Prof. F.W.K. Müller. The beginning of the story is missing, so it starts with the Sages or Magi already in Palestine, meeting King Herod.

**The legend of "The Stone of the Wise Men and the Child Jesus":**

.....At the time of Herod the Tetrach, the Magi were declaring their intentions to him in Jerusalem. They declared humbly, "We wish to find His great Majesty, and to praise Him". In response Herod commanded that they diligently pursue their goal". He said, "Now, my beloved sons, set forth ! Be diligent ! Search ! Enquire ! Once you have found Him, return here to me, tell me about Him, for I will go also and praise Him". Whereupon those sages went journeying forth from Jerusalem, and a star went with them. When the sages reached Bethlehem, the star stayed still and proceeded no further. Soon thereafter the Magi found the Messiah, the divine One.

Trembling, they walked ever nearer to their journey's end, entering into the place where the Messiah was born. They unrolled their luggage packs, and brought forth the gifts which they had brought. Three kinds of gifts: gold, myrrh and also incense. They did homage to Him, praising and blessing Him, the Lord and ruler, the divine Messiah. Those sages thought as they entered His presence, "As this is the Son of God, He will receive incense. If He is a king He shall receive the gold. If He is the Healer, He shall receive the healing balsam of myrrh." So speaking they laid their gifts upon a plate and brought it to Him. The Magi yearned to know His thoughts, the thoughts of the son of the eternal God, the royal Messiah; would he be pleased with the gifts? He was indeed pleased with all three kinds of gifts, and received all three.

To the sages he spoke: "O Magi, you and your three kinds of thoughts have entered into this place; The Son of God am I, a ruler also am I, and a healer too, am I." Thus further did He say, "Depart in good cheer, released from your troubles." However, the sages had knocked off a segment from the corner of His stone crib as they gathered around Him; from this the Messiah broke off a clump of stone with His hand and presented it to them. As they departed from that place, they found they could scarcely lift or hold the stone, their horses also were unable to carry it hence. They therefore held counsel, and said, "This stone is extremely heavy, whatever this clump of stone really is, neither we nor our beasts can carry it. We won't be able to carry it away with us."

However as there was a spring in the vicinity, they toiled with it across to the well, and dropped it into the water. Proceeding on their way, they had not gone far when what did they see? In the well, a vast radiance, suffused with fiery flashes of light, was glowing from the well; a light rose up into the blue ether, and stayed stationary there. As they gazed at the wondrous sign, the sages began to understand and recognize what it meant. Falling to the ground in fear, they began to pray. Later on they spoke amongst themselves, full of regret saying, "He had given to us a sacred stone, a most worshipful gem, we were alas, unworthy of this honour. For we did not recognize it, and have dropped it into a well." Then the Angel of the Lord appeared to them, and guided them into other pathways, that they did not return to Herod.... [77]

The connection of the Philosopher's Stone with the Christ-force and the physical world, is presented here in a simple, yet powerful way. It points to the power of Christ, as the Lord of Life,

---

[77] *Die Anbetung der Magier.* **Uigurica**; in, Abhandlung der Königlich Preussischen Akademie der Wissenschaften, 1908.

the Bread of Life, to transform and refine the physical world. This is due to the Life-Spirit; that is, cosmic Life-Spirit of the Christ, which imbued with the divine higher aspects of the ethers, can revive and renew these etheric forces of creation and hence the physical world. Such divine powers can not be endured by humans normally; high spiritual development is needed for that. That this activity from within the ethers is implied here, is affirmed by another wonderful initiatory text from the Manichaeans. This text dates from about AD 350 and was found in Egypt in the Coptic language; it is a hymn in praise of God, but meaning that through the Christ, God's divine powers could become manifest in our world. It is actually referring to the four ethers that sustain our world,

> ....He established Dwellings of Life and set up living images in them which never perish:
> he evoked Clouds of Brightness, from which descend dew and life;
> he summoned a holy Fire, which gives a fragrant burning;
> he evoked a Wind and Air, which breathe the breath of the living ;
> he evoked holy Mountains from which arise fragrant roots...[78]

The first line here appears to refer to an overall renewal of creation. Then, in the second line, are references to the Water-ether or Tone-ether, from which dew and rain literally precipitate out, giving life to the parched world. Then the Warmth-ether is referred to, from which heat, fire and seeds derive their existence. Then the light-ether, which permeates the winds and the air. Lastly, the Life-ether is referred to, from which solid, dense matter is formed.[79]

The implication of this ancient Manichaean text is the same as the Rosicrucian attitude to the Philosopher's Stone that we saw earlier: namely that it is the etheric forces in creation which sustain and maintain the physical world, and it is these which the spiritually-minded alchemist is seeking to experience. This theme links to the explanation that Rudolf Steiner gave for the Philosopher's Stone. The alchemists' description of the Stone varies considerably, and how to prepare such a reality – highly treasured by all three types of alchemists – was kept veiled. Rudolf Steiner explains that the Philosopher's Stone, from the point of view of spiritual development, is in effect a non-tangible form of carbon, which will underlie the physical body, in its redeemed form, in the far future. This shall be a transparent body, which Rudolf Steiner refers to as a "diamond body"; and the forming of this is assisted by certain meditative breathing exercises.[80] Rudolf Steiner taught that if this breathing process is undertaken successfully, then the mineralised, physical body will become more ethereal; this is the transparent 'diamond body'.

**The Philosophers' Stone**
Rudolf Steiner also made a brief comment in regard to the meditative breathing exercises, that this is an activity "that involves the "I" exerting an influence into the physical body of the human being, so as to assist the gradual emergence of this mysterious third aspect of our spirit; the Spirit-human or Atma (also spelt as 'Atman'). According to Rudolf Steiner, 'Atman' comes from 'Atmen', the German word for breathing;[81] 'Atman' is an alternative name for the mysterious Spirit-human. So the matrass in the painting, which has some substance inside it undergoing a refining process, is probably placed here as a symbol of the physical body entering into a process of refinement, which releases the Spirit-human. As Rudolf Steiner told one audience, "The human being itself is that retort...which becomes transformed."[82]

Just what kind of different existence human beings will be experiencing in the far future, when this process of producing the Philosophers' Stone is achieved, is not explained. He mentions

---

[78] *Manichaean Psalm-Book*, Pt.2, edit. C.R.C. p. 208, Allberry Kohlhammer Vlg, Stuttgart, 1938.
[79] For a clear presentation on the 4 ethers permeating specific layers of our atmosphere, see my *Rudolf Steiner Handbook*.
[80] GA 55, p. 200 & GA 57, p.154.

[81] GA 55, p. 201, and GA 59, p.15 and GA 142, p.16.
[82] GA 55, p.101.

briefly that an initiate who learns to develop the Philosophers' Stone, "transforms the cosmos", meaning the planetary spheres become refined through such a sacred achievement, because the human soul is an extract of these spheres.[83] Also when he refers to the Philosophers' Stone, he mentions a goal that lies nearer at hand, and which is an integral part of the painting: approaching the Holy Grail. He explains that the meditant who is working on the refining of the body, in this subtle way through meditation associated with breathing, becomes able to "receive the holy love-lance" of the Grail legends, referring to the rays of spiritual light from the sun.

We have seen earlier, that the Philosophers' Stone is associated with the events of Golgotha in a legend created by the Manichaeans, and there is a matrass at the top of the new Tree of Life. But what is the association of this alchemical process with the Mystery of Golgotha, which is depicted so dramatically in the crucifixion scene below ? There appears to be nothing said by Rudolf Steiner about this theme, but the refining of the physical body implies making it less 'hardened' or less mineralized; and this in turn implies that the underlying force-structure that keeps the body intact, called "the phantom" (meaning a tenuous, spectral form) by Rudolf Steiner, is being assisted. Rudolf Steiner explains that, invisible behind the matter in the body's cells, is a 'force-structure', produced by the gods long ago in the Saturn aeon. He also explains that it is an etheric form, created in the 'First Elemental Realm', which contains the Idea of all mineral-physical things. This 'force-structure' does have a physical presence; this is sustained from Devachan.[84]

This 'phantom' is harmed by the presence of mineralized or physical matter in the body, which Rudolf Steiner calls "ash"; it has become somewhat degenerated by the ash. This underlying archetype of the body is included in what the cosmic Christ specifically set out, with regard to humanity, to save from future degeneration, by the sacrifices on Golgotha. Rudolf Steiner reports, that to achieve this, at the Mystery of Golgotha, a germinal form of this archetypal force-structure was sent out into every human being.[85] The Atma or Spirit-human could not be developed in the future, if the physical body and its underlying archetypal reality, were not saved from further degenerating.[86]

This theme can appear somewhat abstract and theoretical, but the renewal of the physical body will be a crucial element in humanity's future, and it is this very process which became a key teaching in Christianity, where it is known as the 'bodily resurrection of Christ'. Of course, in Christian theology, there is no knowledge of the esoteric meaning of this phrase, and this has led to the erroneous conclusion that people shall exist for ever in Heaven, in a kind of improved physical (flesh) body. But it is not the flesh body that shall be preserved for the future, but rather the underlying energy-structure sustaining our body, the so-called 'phantom'. We shall encounter this theme again in the picture.

### Initiatory secrets in the Greek New Testament
This topic in fact is about an especially crucial theme, for Rudolf Steiner's teachings about this, reveal the astonishing situation that none of the pre-Golgotha initiates were able to arise fully to the Spirit-human stage. This they could only achieve after the cosmic Christ brought about this mighty redemption process for the physical body.[87] And it is precisely this profound truth which is presented in the initiatory level of meaning in the Greek text, of a sentence in St. Matthew's Gospel, 27:51-53. This extraordinary passage has remained a complete enigma to theologians throughout the centuries, and is consequently avoided in sermons,

---

[83] GA 99, lecture, 6th June 1907, and in lectures given at the 1907 Munich Conference (GA 284/85).
[84] GA 153, p.72. See his book, *Theosophy* for more about the "Elemental Realms".
[85] GA 141, p.57.
[86] So it can be concluded that the spiritualizing of the body through the alchemical Philosophers' Stone breathing exercises, directly assists the attaining of the Atma or Spirit-human.

[87] GA 131, *From Jesus to Christ*, 11th Oct. 1911.

> <sup>Mt 27:51</sup> At that moment the curtain of the temple was torn in two from top to bottom. The earth shook and the rocks split.
> <sup>Mt 27:52</sup> The tombs broke open and the bodies of many holy people who had died were raised to life.
> <sup>Mt 27:53</sup> They came out of the tombs, and after Jesus' resurrection they went into the holy city and appeared to many people.

The hidden meanings are not clear in this NIV translation; and here I cannot go into all the details, that will be done in a future book. But we note that the verb in the phrase, "...and *appeared* to many people" tells the esoteric scholar that the event described is happening on a non-material, invisible level, and is about the phantom or archetypal body. This is because the verb, 'emthanizo' (ἐμθανίζω) has been used here especially, instead of a normal verb for 'seeing'; the verb used here occurs in Hellenistic literature for 'the becoming perceptible of a deity to mortals'.

That this mysterious process is occurring on a spiritual plane, and not in the physical world, is further indicated by the expression, 'holy city', instead of the name 'Jerusalem'. This is a veiled way of referring to the 'heavenly Jerusalem', that is, the astral-devachanic celestial Jerusalem. It is discreetly indicated in the Bible that above the physical Jerusalem is a heavenly dwelling place of divine beings associated with the Messiah. This is also the only place in St. Matthew's Gospel, where he uses the word 'hagion' (ἁγίων) to refer to 'holy ones' (that is, initiates).

### The Three, the Twelve and the Four
The highest of the features in this huge painting, directly above the new Tree of Life, is a triangle, below which are twelve column-like forms and below these are four elongated oval shapes, see illustration 18. From the triangle, rays of light spread out, touching Buddha, the Ark of the Covenant and reaching Melchizedek, on the left side, On the right side the light streams out across Lazaros-John to the dove, as a symbol of the Holy Spirit, and on to the figure of the Spirit-self (the woman with the sun in the middle and the moon beneath her feet). The three shapes above the tree represent the divine beings and cosmic forces operative in the Great Work of evolving humanity into a life-wave, (rescued from the material realm where Lucifer and Ahriman have their power), up into a Spirit-self humanity of the Jupiter aeon.

The triangle represents the Godhead, the triune divine source of creation, and beneath it, the twelve columns represent the zodiac, which has a definite role in the Bible, from the 12 tribes of Israel through to the 12 disciples and finally the 12-sided heavenly Jerusalem. The four shapes below the zodiac appear to represent the fourfold aspect to our world: the fourfold human being of physical, etheric, astral and ego. But these four can also point to the four ethers from which the four states of matter arise. Before we explore the last third of the painting, it will be helpful to consider the nature of the spiritual beings in the upper area of the painting, near to the Principalities, extending both to the left and to the right.

As Anna May informs us, these are Archangels, and they represent the theme of the seven Archangels who exert a cultural influence on humanity, during each of the 2,160 year zodiacal Ages. For practical reasons, there are not seven Archangels depicted for each of the two Principalities. Also, we need to note that there is an unusual feature associated with the faces and heads of these Archangels: what appears to be flames arise up from their foreheads. This refers to the alternative name given to them by Rudolf Steiner, the "Spirits of Fire"; this is because in the remote evolutionary Moon aeon, these beings were active helping higher beings induce astrality (that is, desires, pleasure and pain, etc.) in human beings. Now a careful look at this fantastical section of the painting shows a very interesting feature: there are two instances of an Archangel who appears to be what we could call 'burdened' by a task.

### The burdened Archangels
Looking at the upper area of the painting to the left of 'Pharao', and also to the right of 'Hellas', various Archangels are depicted; see illustration 19. In the process of refreshing the painting, I could see a previously un-noticed feature. On the left, and over on the right, there is an

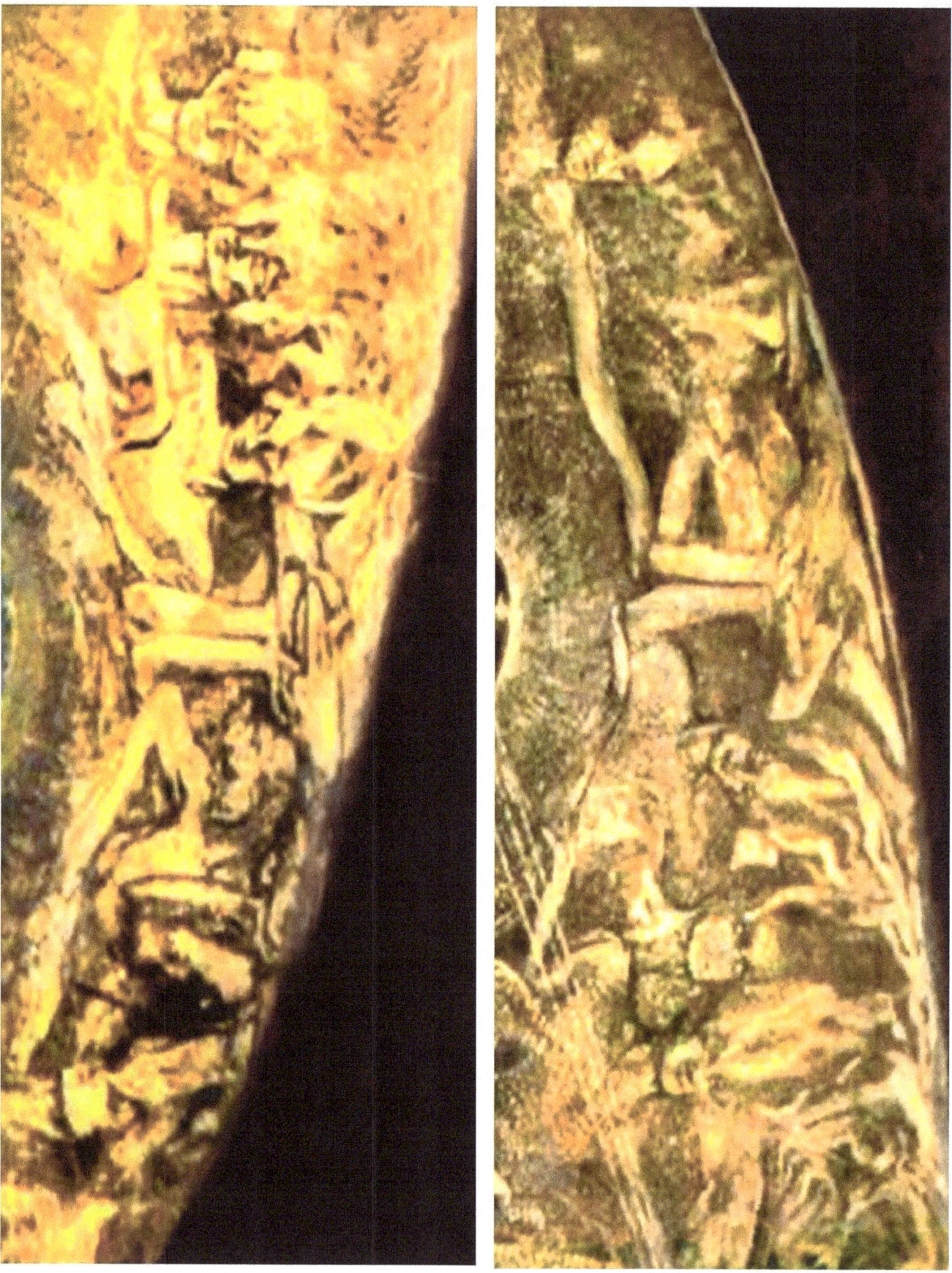

19 The Archangels, left and right of the central section

Archangel who is strenuously active, helping humanity, at a crucial time. These times are when a Time-spirit hands over his rulership to the next Time-spirit. At these points, the Archangel involved is depicted as bent over; see illustration 20. So who are these two 'burdened' Archangels? We know from Rudolf Steiner that the seven planetary Archangels each have a Regency, which occur in a regular sequence; during any Regency, the Archangel exerts a subtle influence on the inner life of human beings. Each Regency lasts about 350 years; some are only 320-340 years in length, although the Sun Archangel Regency lasts about 460 years.

To determine who these two Archangels are in the upper part of the painting, we need to note the year when the Age of 'Pharao' began, this is, the Egyptian-Mesopotamian Age, because one of these bent-over Archangels is placed just before this Age began, in 2907 BC. We also need to note when the Greco-Latin Age or the Age of Hellas ended, because the other bent-over Archangel is placed just after this Age ended; this was in AD 1413. Then we superimpose the dates of the Regencies of the Archangels onto the flow of history encompassing this period of time; which means from about 3,300 BC to AD 1500. In calculating the dates for these Regencies back to the beginning of the Age of Taurus (2907 BC) we can not be perhaps fully exact, as Rudolf Steiner did not give the precise dates for this earlier epoch. But with regard to the more recent times, he indicated how long these Regencies last; so we can reasonably deduce that these lengths of time for any Regency also applied to the earlier epoch.

So in attempting to ascertain which Archangels are involved here, we can be confident that the margin of error will be quite small. For the ancient Egyptian-Mesopotamian Age, we discover that the Regency of Gabriel ended a little before the era of 'Pharao' began, which was in 2907 BC (the Age of Taurus). In fact, our calculations show that the Regency of Gabriel would have started approximately in 3550 BC, and ended about 3200 BC. Since the Age of Michael follows that of Gabriel, it follows that this Michael Regency started a little before the time of 'Pharao' (the Age of Taurus), in fact around 3200, and lasted until about 2750 BC.

For the more recent era, the timing of the Regency of an Archangel for the epoch when the Age of 'Hellas' ended (the Greco-Latin Age) and thus the Fifth Post-Atlantean Age began, is easier to know, as Rudolf Steiner gives the precise dates for this period. Gabriel reigned between 1510-1879 AD, and then Michael's reign began, in 1879, this shall continue until about 2340-60 AD. Illustration 19 shows the busy, complex activity of Archangels, extending both left and right of the centre of the picture, however these two burdened Archangels don't stand out strongly in this maze of beings. Illustration 20 however shows them more clearly, highlighting each one, and placing them near to a time-scale diagram, that makes clear the timing of their Regencies within the context of the zodiac ages or cultural epochs.

**Archangel Michael versus Lucifer, 3000 BC**
What all this means is that in the painting, the burdened Archangel on the left, where 'Pharao' is starting to reign, (his hand is grasping that of another, earlier Principality), is in fact, Archangel Michael. For this Archangel is facing towards 'Pharao', and is placed before the Age of Taurus begins. So this Archangel's Regency commences a little before the time of 'Pharao' begins, the epoch governed by the Folk-spirit of ancient Egypt. As illustration 20 shows, Michael's regency extends from about 3,200 BC to about 2750 BC. What caused a burden for Michael back then was a remarkable event, about which however Rudolf Steiner said very little. He taught about 3000 BC, Lucifer 'incarnated'; that is, he over-shadowed a person. This was someone who was living in China at that time. This extraordinary event coincides with the Regency of Michael.

It was around 2,900 BC, which is about 200-300 years after the Regency of Michael began, that Lucifer began to exert a potent influence on humanity, in an endeavour to lead people off into unwholesome states of consciousness. Rudolf Steiner did not disclose anything about the dynamics and challenges of that earlier Michaelic Regency, but this situation appears to be why a 'burdened' Archangel is placed there in the painting. From this, we can conclude that Michael, who is now combating Ahriman in our times, had been combating Lucifer some 5,000 years ago. This means that Archangel Michael has been helping humanity since long ago. He is represented in this painting three times; here as a burdened helper of the Time-Spirit, then near to the cross on Golgotha, and thirdly, as we shall see, he is to be seen on the far right of the painting.

# The Right Side

## Archangel Gabriel

Over in the last third of the triptych, high up in the right side of the painting; there is another burdened Archangel. This one is facing back, towards the Christ-event in the centre of the picture. This Archangel is placed just after the Age of Aries governed by 'Hellas', has ended and the Age of Pisces began. This is where the hand of 'Hellas' is reaching out to the hand of another Time-Spirit; this was in AD 1413. As illustration 20 shows, the Regency of Archangel Gabriel began about 100 years after the reign of 'Hellas' ended and the Age of Pisces began; actually in AD 1510. Rudolf Steiner mentioned this Regency of Gabriel in some detail. He taught that during her Regency,[88] Gabriel had the task of assisting cosmic influences on the etheric level, which were intending to produce subtle refinements or changes in the human brain. These cosmic forces were affecting the configuration of the brain's structure in a manner that would orient human thinking more to the physical world. He mentioned that it was actually a result of this activity that the scientific attitude to the physical world arose in the western world.[89] He explains that during this process,

> fine structures were developed in the frontal lobe of the brain, and this became an inherited feature, so that people then began to be born with such a development.[90]

So, generations of people incarnating into the western world would have this capacity incorporated in their physical-etheric heredity. It is significant to note here, that as the next Regency began, that of Archangel Michael, those same cosmic forces would become free to assist the human being to be a vessel for the kind of thinking that enables people to become intuitive; to grasp spiritual ideas. It is precisely this kind of consciousness that Archangel Michael now seeks to strengthen in humanity. This is a kind of thinking which is spiritually open or 'holistic', yet not flighty, not wanting to indulge in fanciful ideas, but to sense the link between the physical world and the higher realms which sustain it.[91] In other words, during the Regency of Archangel Michael, human beings can have an opportunity, if they so will, to experience spiritual truths in the form of intuitive insights and perhaps as direct clairvoyant perceptions.

However, during the Regency of Gabriel, who was intending to bring about a consciousness more focused on the physical world, strong Luciferic influences were set in motion specifically to oppose her efforts. The intention of these Luciferic spirits was to hinder this work of Archangel Gabriel and bring about later, in the Regency of Michael, attitudes in people concerning the spiritual worlds, which would be strongly un-grounded. This would result in luciferic attitudes to the spiritual aspect of life, from which all sorts of mystical cults would be formed. People attracted to these groups would succumb to the temptation to use (or revive) the old, inappropriate, psychic tendencies of the past. In his *Letters to Members* in 1924, Rudolf Steiner refers to this opposition of Luciferic spirits to Gabriel.

It appears reasonable to conclude that, on the right side of the painting, as an expression of these inner spiritual dynamics in history, Archangel Gabriel is depicted as an Archangel burdened by the effort to combat these luciferic influences. Lucifer beings who were opposing the process of making subtle refinements to the brain.[92]

---

[88] The Archangel Gabriel is experienced by the initiate as having a similar quality to 'femininity'; in Rudolf Steiner description, this is a being with "a lofty, lovely quality". (GA 265, p.337).
[89] GA 146, p. 86.
[90] GA 152, p.57
[91] GA 152, lecture 18th May, 1913 & GA 146 lecture 1st June 1913.
[92] GA 26, p. 122, the Michael Mystery/ Leading Thoughts of 23rd Nov. 1924.

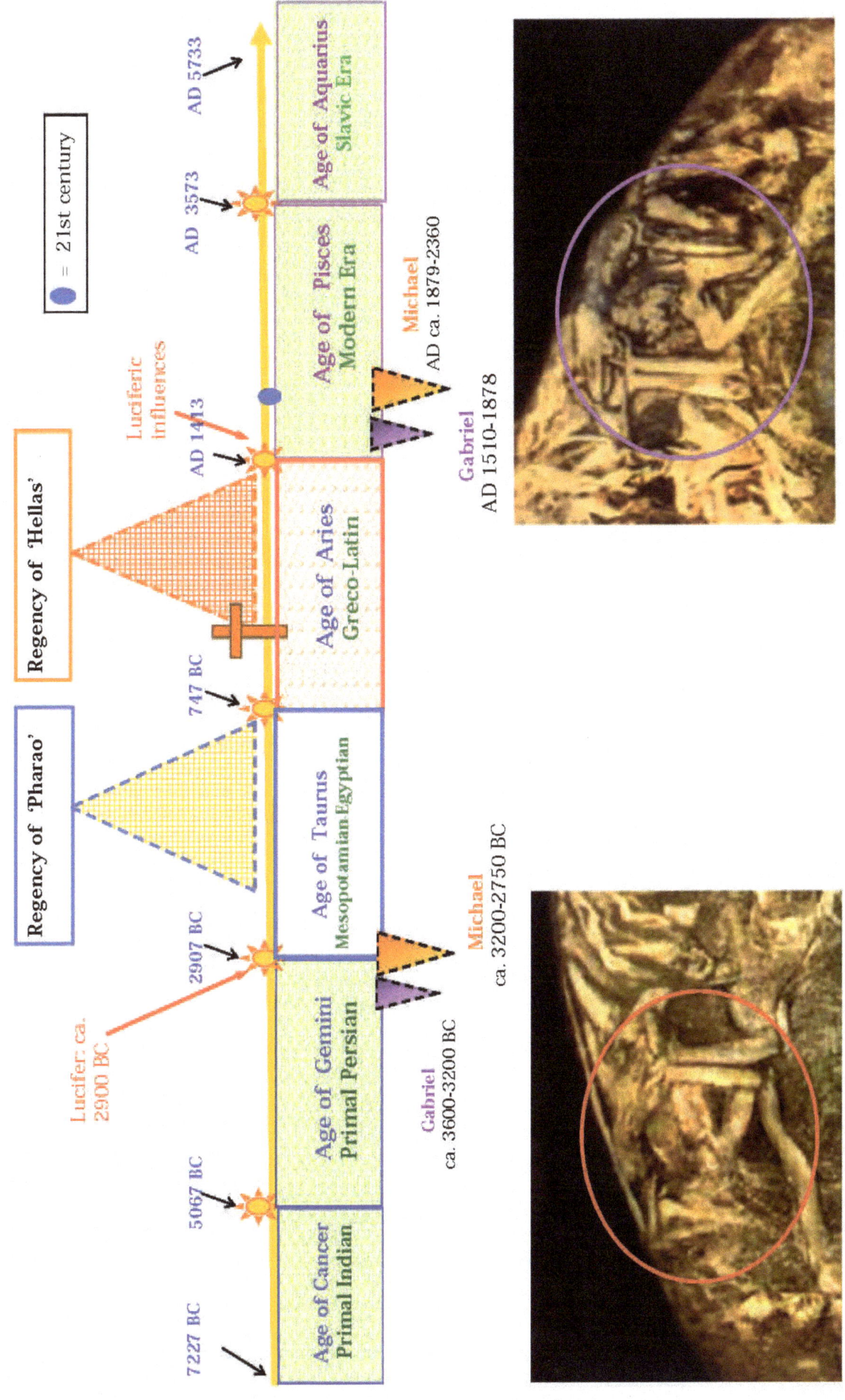

**20 The 'burdened' Archangels:** Understanding the two Time-spirits and the burdened archangel, Gabriel. Left: Just before 'Pharoa' becomes the Time-spirit, Lucifer 'incarnates' and Michael battles against this. Right: Just after 'Hellas' ceases to be the Time-spirit, Gabriel battles against Luciferic influences.

**The Right Side** (continued)

**In AD 1250: the initiation of Christian Rosencreutz**
Now we turn our attention to the striking central scene of the right sector of the painting, see illustration 21. This is the scene below the descending dove, representing the Holy Spirit: this is the scene which depicts an initiation process which could be called a ceremony, that occurred in the year 1250 AD. This process took place in a remote place in Europe, and the focus of the ceremony is the young person lying on an unusual pedestal, surrounded by a group of people. This holy person had been Lazaros-John and he shall be known as Christian Rosencreutz in the next century, as a direct outcome of this ceremony. The way this scene has been designed, it has the quality of being a counterpart to the temple scene with Solomon, the Queen of Sheba and Hiram. The two outermost people, holding their standards of flags, create a definite sculptural quality to the event, giving it a distinct form, and create a balancing counterpart to the effect of Solomon and Hiram, in the left side of the painting.

So central is this event to the painting, and the understanding of Rosicrucianism, that it is necessary here to provide Rudolf Steiner's own words about this; here is a long quote from a lecture given in 1911, and probably attended by Anna May:

> In a place in Europe that cannot be named yet – though this will be possible in the not very distant future – a lodge of a very spiritual nature was formed comprising a council of twelve men who had received into themselves the sum of the spiritual wisdom of olden times and of their own time. So we are concerned with twelve men who lived in that dark era, twelve outstanding individualities, who united together to help the progress of humanity. None of them could see directly into the spiritual world, but they could awaken to life in themselves memories of what they had experienced through earlier initiations. And the karma of mankind brought it about that in seven of the twelve, all that still remained to mankind of the ancient Atlantean epoch was incarnated. In my *Occult Science* it has already been stated that in the seven holy Rishis of old, the teachers of the ancient Indian cultural epoch, all that was left of the Atlantean epoch was preserved.
>
> These seven men who were incarnated again in the thirteenth century, and who were part of the council of twelve, were just those who could look back into the seven streams of the ancient Atlantean cultural epoch of mankind, and the further course of these streams. Among these seven individualities each one of them could bring one stream to life for their time and the present time. In addition to these seven there were another four who could not look back into times long past but could look back to the occult wisdom mankind had acquired in the four post-Atlantean epochs. The first could look back to the ancient Indian period, the second to the ancient Persian cultural period, the third to the Egyptian-Chaldean-Assyrian-Babylonian cultural period and the fourth to the Greco-Roman culture. These four joined the seven to form a council of wise men in the thirteenth century.
>
> A twelfth had the fewest memories as it were, however he was the most intellectual among them, and it was his task to foster external science in particular. These twelve individualities not only lived in the experiences of Western esotericism, but these twelve different streams of wisdom worked together to make a whole. The seven successors of the seven Rishis remembered their ancient wisdom, and the other five represented the wisdom of the five post-Atlantean cultures. Thus the twelve represented the whole of Atlantean and post-Atlantean wisdom. The twelfth was a man who attained the intellectual wisdom of his time in the highest degree. He possessed intellectually all the knowledge of his time, whilst the others, to whom direct spiritual wisdom was also denied at that time, acquired their knowledge by returning in memory to their earlier incarnations.
>
> The beginning of a new culture was only possible, however, because a thirteenth came to join the twelve. The thirteenth did not become a scholar in the accepted sense of that

time. He was an individuality who had been incarnated at the time of the Mystery of Golgotha. In the incarnations that followed he prepared himself for his mission through humility of soul and through a fervent life devoted to God. He was a great soul, a pious, deeply mystical human being, who had not just acquired these qualities but was born with them. If you imagine to yourselves a young man who is very pious and who devotes all his time to fervent prayer to God, then you can have a picture of the individuality of this thirteenth. He grew up entirely under the care and instruction of the twelve, and he received as much wisdom as each one could give him. He was educated with the greatest care, and every precaution was taken to see that no one other than the twelve exercised an influence on him.

He was kept apart from the rest of the world. He was a very delicate child in that incarnation of the thirteenth century, and therefore the education that the twelve bestowed upon him worked right into his physical body. Now the twelve, being deeply devoted to their spiritual tasks and inwardly permeated with Christianity, were conscious that the external Christianity of the Church was only a caricature of the real Christianity. They were permeated with the greatness of Christianity, although in the outside world they were taken to be its enemies. Each individuality worked his way into just one aspect of Christianity. Their endeavour was to unite the various religions into one great whole. They were convinced that the whole of spiritual life was contained in their twelve streams, and each one influenced the pupil to the best of his ability. Their aim was to achieve a synthesis of all the religions, but they knew that this was not to be achieved by means of any theory, but only as the result of spiritual life. And for this a suitable education of the thirteenth was essential.

Whilst the spiritual forces of the thirteenth increased beyond measure, his physical forces drained away. It came to the point where he almost ceased to have any further connection with external life, and all interest in the physical world disappeared. He lived entirely for the sake of the spiritual development which the twelve were bringing about in him. The wisdom of the twelve was reflected in him. It reached the point where the thirteenth refused to eat and wasted away. Then an event occurred that could only happen once in history. It was the kind of event that can take place when the forces of the macrocosm co-operate for the sake of what they can bring to fruition. After a few days the body of the thirteenth became quite transparent, and for days he lay as though dead.

The twelve now gathered round him at certain intervals; at these moments all knowledge and wisdom flowed from their lips. Whilst the thirteenth lay as though dead, they let their wisdom flow towards him in short prayer-like formulae. The best way to imagine them is to picture the twelve in a circle round the thirteenth. This situation ended when the soul of the thirteenth awakened like a new soul. He had experienced a great transformation of soul. Within it there now existed something that was like a completely new birth of the twelve streams of wisdom, so that the twelve wise men could also learn something entirely new from the youth. His body, too, came to life now in such a way that this revival of his absolutely transparent body was beyond compare. The youth could now speak of quite new experiences.

The twelve could recognise that he had experienced the event of Damascus: it was a repetition of the vision of Paul on the road to Damascus. In the course of a few weeks the thirteenth reproduced all the wisdom he had received from the twelve, but in a new form. This new form was as though given by Christ Himself. What he now revealed to them, the twelve called true Christianity, the synthesis of all the religions, and they distinguished between this true Christianity and the Christianity of the period in which they lived. The thirteenth died relatively young, and the twelve then devoted themselves to the task of

**21 The Initiation scene in AD 1250:** The Wisdom of the Ages is received by the youth and transformed in the Christ-light.

recording what the thirteenth had revealed to them, in 'imaginations' {i.e., astral imagery} – for it could only be done in that way.[93]

This priceless revelation from Rudolf Steiner gives the meditant substantial help in contemplating the importance and sanctity of Christian Rosencreutz. It is from the influence of these astral images, mentioned in this lecture, in the consciousness of this group of twelve and their students, enhanced by the inspiration from Christian Rosencreutz, which led to esoteric images being painted on the walls of the extraordinary upper chapel in castle Karlstejn, near Prague, which date from the 14th century. A castle which Rudolf Steiner visited, and during this visit confirmed that the now-faded 14th century paintings in the chapel are indeed connected to Christian Rosencreutz. In the following centuries, a variety of esoteric symbols were in use amongst Rosicrucian groups, which eventually became known as the 'secret symbols of the Rosicrucians'; these also have their origin in this holy ceremony of AD 1250. Rudolf Steiner taught that by the 18th century, these symbols had been betrayed, and came into the hands of people who were not granted access to the secretive Order, as the original Rosicrucian movement faded away.

**The Dove and the Holy Spirit**
In many ways, all of this holiness proceeding from Christian Rosencreutz is represented by the prominent white dove within a heavenly blue and golden halo, descending towards the sarcophagus. The dove is of course a very well known symbol in Christianity of the Holy Spirit, and derives from the report in the Gospels of how, at the Baptism of Jesus, the Spirit descended upon Jesus, as if in the form of a dove. In the painting, the dove is the new counter-part to the Old Testament's Ark of the Covenant, in which God resided as it were. The term 'Holy Spirit' is not explained as such in the Bible; Rudolf Steiner explained it from various perspectives and this reveals that the term is multi-faceted.

It is an outpouring from the spiritual worlds, and this results in the Spirit-self forming in the human being; both the Spiritual-self together with the beginnings of the Life-Spirit in the etheric body.[94] It derives from the Christ-light that permeates the Earth's aura since the Resurrection.[95] As it forms in the human being, that person's previously rudimentary devachanic aura becomes larger, empowered and intensely radiant.[96] But a deeply sacred aspect of the Holy Spirit is that the result of the receiving of the Holy Spirit – in this immensely powerful initiatory sense – is that the human being becomes part of a new 'Group-soul'. Not one of the four apocalyptic group-souls which the sarcophagus in this scene depicts, but a new 'Group-soul-community' which is part of the extended spiritual being-ness of Christ Jesus; so it is a 'Christéd community'.[97]

**The celestial forces operative in the year AD 1250**
Underlying the initiation process there is here the activity of a sublime spiritual being in the sun-sphere, whose influence becomes especially strong in either hemisphere of our planet during the wintertime, that is in the 12-day Yuletide or Holy Nights. As I have shown in my book, *Living a Spiritual Year*, it is during the Holy Nights of either hemisphere that the soul can draw near to Christ Jesus, whilst out of the body in sleep, and thus be permeated by Life-spirit forces from the cosmic Christ.

A passage referring to this occurrence in the Holy Nights is especially placed inside the Shakespearean play, *Hamlet*, although it is not necessary for the play. And in this passage we can detect the inspiring influence of the great Christian Rosencreutz, for his own transformative

---
[93] GA 130, lect. Neuchatel, 27.Sept. 1911.
[94] GA 94, p. 291.
[95] GA 112. p.29 and GA 118, p. 170
[96] See my *The Way to the Sacred* for more about the Devachanic aura.
[97] GA 98, ps. 99-101.

initiation occurred in the year when the Holy Nights radiance was stronger than it had been for thousands of years,[98]

> *Some say 'gainst that season wherein the Saviour's birth is celebrated, no witch does take....so hallow'd and so gracious is the time.*

As Rudolf Steiner taught,

> The Christmas-Holy Nights time is bound to processes in the earth. For the human being, together with the earth {that is, the hemisphere} undergoes the 'Christmas-Holy Nights alteration' of the hemisphere.

Because of the seasonal process, each winter brings about an increased presence of the sacred Life-spirit forces from the sun gods, this is then taken up and utilised by the Christ, making the Yuletide so holy. Because both hemispheres have a wintertime, Rudolf Steiner revealed in a lecture in Oslo that the Holy Nights occur in both hemispheres in their respective winter time,

> ....just consider, though, that when we here {in Europe} have St. John's festival; that is, when it is the case that our souls can follow the Earth-soul which {now} arises and 'unites' itself with the stars, **then the Antipodes, the Antipodeans, have their Christmas-Holy Nights.**[99]

To ensure that his audience grasped that the Holy Nights are caused by the seasonal processes, and not mystically induced globally by the religious calendar, he emphasized this seasonal aspect, saying,

> ...in regard to the meeting with Christ Jesus {in winter}, this occurrence **is an integral aspect of the *seasonal cycle* of the year**. If it were not united to the seasonal cycle of the year, then the {impossible} result would be, that one person could celebrate a Christmas-Holy Nights in December, another person in March, and so on... in regard to this Meeting, which is placed in the cycle of the natural year, and there the human being is also placed....in direct connection with the natural cycle of the year. **In this matter the human being is placed within the *natural cycle* of the year**....[100]     (emphasis mine AA)

Now this theme is very relevant to our painting, because, as we earlier noted, if we look at the zodiac near Moses, we see an odd feature near the symbol for Capricorn. Two white energy lines radiate down to it from a holy centre in the 'menorah-bush', where the Hebrew words spoken to Moses are placed. In other words, a high spiritual energy from the cosmic Christ and Jahveh, are radiating into Capricorn, in some way. What this feature is signifying is that the Holy Nights – in the northern hemisphere – occur in the time when the sun is in the sign of Capricorn, and that in the year AD 1250, this solar influence from Capricorn shall be at the strongest it has been for thousands of years.

For Rudolf Steiner told an audience, during the Holy Nights of 1910, whilst referring to the Rosicrucians, that in the year AD 1250, the sun itself was at perigee at the winter solstice of the northern hemisphere, during the Holy Nights (whilst the sun was in the sign of Capricorn). This means that the sun was at its closest position to the Earth.[101] This especially powerful celestial alignment had not happened since about 9,200 BC. He explains that, as a result of this, the Powers, or Spirits of Form, were more active in the human soul than they had been for millennia.[102] This is the reason why the exceptional initiation process for Christian Rosencreutz occurred in that year.

---

[98] Actually since 9,200 BC.
[99] When he says "unites itself with the stars" he is being poetic, re-phrasing what he said a few minutes earlier, that "the earth-soul {in that hemisphere} strives upwards, towards the stars". (GA 226, p.204)
[100] GA 175, lect. 27th Feb. 1917, p. 79, "..es ist ...gebunden an die Naturordnung..in unmittelbar Zusammenhang mit dem Naturlaufe.."
[101] GA 126 *Occult History*, lecture 31st Dec. 1910.
[102] GA 130, Lecture 29th Jan. 1911.

**22 Royal Arch Tracing Board** with sarcophagus, an arch, the four Apocalyptic life-forms, the symbol for God hovering above, and also some zodiac signs.

## Royal Arch Freemasonry

Before we explore how this painting depicts this event of AD 1250, and which personalities are shown here, we need to be aware that once again a Freemasonry element is interwoven into the painting. There is a type of Masonry known as degree 'Royal Arch' Masonry, and as with other degrees, its historical origin is unknown, but seemed to have begun in the early 1700's. The themes of its rituals are, in common with other Masonic rites, drawn from the Old Testament. It has its own specific ornaments that are used to decorate the lodge during ceremonies held for its four degrees.

A significant feature of this 'chapter' of Freemasonry is an initiatory sarcophagus, often on a pedestal, and representations of the four primal creatures, and also a chequered floor pattern called a 'tracing board' or floor cloth; see illustration 22. All of these freemasonry features are present here in the depiction of the initiation of the youth, although in a metamorphosed way. There are also seven stars, or seven planets; it is unknown which is meant, but if it refers to planets then this is also present in our painting, in that the seven Rishis are related to the seven classical planets of astrology.[103] If these seven refer to stars, then they are likely to be the Pleiades, which represent Taurus, and Taurus is also a feature of this scene.

The chequered floor pattern and the large, four-sided pedestal are particularly striking Masonic features here. These, and other ornamental features in Royal Arch Masonry are referred to only in very general terms – as is the case in all Freemason ritual texts – but it is understood that they symbolize the 'spiritual re-birth' of the candidate. A primary feature of Freemason lodges is a chequered floor pattern, with various symbolic objects placed on it; this is often reproduced on a ritual apron. The underlying intentions, or esoteric significance of the 'tracing board' is not historically recorded in Freemasonry, but it is generally concluded that this represents the interplay of good and evil in life, in the midst of which the Freemason seeks to progress spiritually. (When I was working on this part of the painting in high magnification, the white squares appeared to have faces drawn within them.)

Only brief words by Rudolf Steiner about the chequered pattern have survived; he identifies this chequered floor pattern which may be present in the lodge as a floor cloth or mosaic tiles, etc., as "the cosmic Plan" (of world evolution) and the black/white segments of this as the "black and white rays in this {the cosmic Plan}."[104] He comments that the commonly used black/white chequerboard for games is a 'profane' popular derivation from the esoteric concept.

On each side there are two people depicted, each with their presence heightened by holding a staff. Why is this? Firstly, they form the necessary boundary to enclose this scene; but looking again at the Royal Arch tracing board, we see that it has two columns. These are of course the columns called Jachin and Boaz, which we commented on earlier. Found between these two columns are the chequered tracing board, the sarcophagus and the 'tetramorph', that is the four-faced, winged entities mentioned in the Apocalypse and the vision of Ezekiel.

## The 'tetramorph' pedestal

In the Royal Arch ornamentations, the four apocalyptic beings: lion, eagle, potential human and bull, are included somewhere in the lodge or on the ritualistic vestments used. In the painting, these four appear as an unusual pedestal which is formed from the tetramorph. Significantly, it is the bull who is facing the viewer. Before we interpret this feature, we need to know that, as Anna May wrote, the youth who is lying above this pedestal, is placed within a transparent, crystalline sarcophagus. There is a link between the prominence of the bull and this transparent sarcophagus.

We should remind ourselves, that earlier we noted the inclusion of Freemason symbols here is for several reasons. Firstly, the lives of initiate Christian Rosencreutz are a major theme. As we

---

[103] GA 108, p. 306.
[104] GA 265 p. 316.

noted earlier, Rudolf Steiner revealed to some small groups of serious students, that Christian Rosencreutz had been Hiram the Master builder, and hence he was involved in an esoteric activity that became a central part of the Freemason tradition. Also, Freemason content enriches the experience of those Theosophists who were involved in the Egyptian Freemasonry, when they contemplated this painting. For those who are not in the Masonic lodges, these Masonic elements also enriched their experience of the painting, because these elements speak powerfully to the soul, which has absorbed some anthroposophical wisdom, even without any knowledge of Freemasonry. For example, the four apocalyptic creatures here, which form the pedestal, tell us that the initiatory process is occurring in a way that shall impact on the fourfold human nature of this youth; that is, his physical body, the etheric body the astral body and the ego-sense. It also tells us that these four parts of the human being have their origin in the four aeons, each of which were influenced by a particular zodiac energy.

**The influence of Taurus**
But in particular, because the bull is prominent here, and the sarcophagus is transparent, we are learning that this initiate, the former Lazaros-John, has specifically overcome the influence of Taurean forces active in human consciousness, since Lemurian times. It is this influence which has been governing our 'ideation', that is the forming of mental images in response to sense perception. To us, this is our normal mental process, but as Rudolf Steiner explains in his Philosophy of Freedom, this mental-imaging process is a consciousness process which is not yet a true 'thinking' process, from which living concepts, often quite sophisticated, are formed.

A concept requires some inner effort from us to be created, and it is meant to embody the real nature of an observed object. As Rudolf Steiner wrote in his Philosophy of Freedom (*The Human Individuality*), "Reality is presented to us as perception and concept, and the subjective representation of this reality, as mental image".[105] The forming of mental images is a process inherent to the incarnate soul, and primarily occurs in response to sensory impressions. This has resulted in a matter-focussed consciousness, and this leads very easily to materialism. In Rudolf Steiner's words,

"Materialism only sees the condensed matter, and has forgotten that, behind the material world there is present the Spiritual – and that above the material things, the Spiritual exists which brings forth matter."[106]

In his lectures on Human and Cosmic Thinking (GA 151), where the 12 zodiac influences on our consciousness are described, Rudolf Steiner allocates 'Rationalism" to Taurus, and he explains that under this influence,

"the human being only lets those ideas have validity which he or she finds, not such ideas which the person may take hold by inner means, through some kind of intuitive or inspirational process; instead only those ideas which the person finds, i.e., 'reads' from observation of sensory-real things."[107]

It was this very process of sensory perception and the consequent forming of mental images, which led to the hardening, or 'mineralizing' of our primordial Lemurian body, which was primarily gelatinous, without any hard mineral component, namely, the skeleton. As the Taurean forces wrought this 'becoming earthly' change in humanity, then the mental ideation (Vorstellung) faculty arose, and precisely as this earth-bound, sensory awareness gathered pace, an enormously significant event occurred. The newly formed particles of mineral substances in the Earth's environs, primarily calcium (called 'ash' by Rudolf Steiner), began to permeate the physical body, hardening it. And this affected the underlying archetypal etheric-physical

---

[105] In the German „Als Wahrnehmung und Begriff stellt sich uns die Wirklichkeit, as Vorstellung die subjektive Repräsentation dieser Wirklicheit."
[106] GA 96 lect. 8th Oct. 1906

[107] GA 151, lect. 21. Jan. 1914.

template of the body, the phantom'. He gave a profound meditative statement about this Taurean influence:

> ...that which the ash thereby pushed into the human body was, from now on, the {kind of dead} thought which transformed the Tone {the cosmic Word resonating in the ether} into words {to express earthly ideas}.
> (*Das*, was die Asche hineindrängt in die menschlichen Leiber, das war nunmehr der *Gedanke*, der den Schall, den Ton, zum Worte macht.) [108]

By 'words', he means, abstract words that serve as ways to express earthly concepts, as human consciousness drew ever more into the material world, as we shall see when we contemplate the bovine image in the painting, near to St. Paul.

In terms of the zodiac, the earthly word-sense, or word-signifying (of our abstract mental pictures), is correlated to Taurus.[109] We note that the Taurean forces that are hardening the body, are an integral part of the process in Lemurian times whereby the planet itself became mineralized. But this process involves gnomes, and to some extent, ahrimanized gnomes, since Ahriman is the being who has a role in the forming of deadened matter out of the ether. It is for this reason that earth-bound thinking is defined in anthroposophical wisdom, as inherently 'ahrimanic'. Here in this scene, we are being told that the initiated youth is reversing this Taurean or 'bull' process; hence the bull figure in the pedestal is facing the viewer, pointing to the task of overcoming the Taurean influence. And this is also why he is placed in a remarkable transparent sarcophagus, as this represents the spiritualized physical body, which is the transparent 'diamond body' of the alchemists.

**The 'diamond body'**
This transparent 'diamond body' is also, from one perspective, the 'Philosopher's Stone'. So in this scene, we are seeing that he who is shortly to become Christian Rosencreutz, has freed his body from the hardened mineral substances or 'ash', and thereby brought renewal to its spectral archetype (or 'phantom'). Rudolf Steiner taught in regard to this,

> The alchemists have always emphasized that the human body in truth consists of the same substance as that of the Philosopher's Stone. The physical body consists actually of an absolutely transparent reality... [110]

So, humanity was sent down into the earth-bound bodily condition by the developing of an earthly consciousness or sense-based thinking, whereby the tone, that is, the cosmic Word resonating in the ether, became only a trigger for concepts and mental images. But to a body-freed consciousness, perception of this cosmic Word results in astral thought-forms (Imaginations) being experienced. To reverse the process whereby an earth-bound consciousness arose, the spiritual seeker has to undertake a meditative training, to gain the ability to hear or perceive the cosmic Word emanating from the zodiac and the planets: and it is exactly this which the painting depicts, in this scene. The youth, in this initiatory process is doing this, as the people gathered around him speak in a mantric way. The outcome of this is that the body becomes spiritualized, or here in fact, quite transparent.

**The group around the sarcophagus**
Firstly, we note that this scene on the right side of the triptych, gives a symmetry to the composition of the painting by balancing the left side, where king Solomon and Hiram form a definite boundary to the Queen of Sheba. On the right side, two people – apparently Joan of Arc and Plato – who are made more prominent by their colour and by holding staffs, frame the scene by forming a boundary. This is an artistic device, the actual scene would not have appeared like this, as these two people were not there, see illustration 23. The sculpting of this scene is a

---

[108] GA 102, p. 94.
[109] See my *Rudolf Steiner Handbook* for more about the 12 senses and the zodiac, and my website for a poster depicting this.
[110] GA 131, p.153.

counter-part to the situation involving Solomon, Hiram and the Queen of Sheba. These three are near to the curtain veiling the entry to the Holy of Holies; but the acolyte in the scene portraying the initiation of AD 1250 is about to become Christian Rosencreutz, so he is no longer outside the Holy of Holies, he is fully within the Divine. He is to be re-born as a person who has received the Holy Spirit to a very profound degree. So there is here a kind of counter-part to the scene in the Temple of Solomon.

Their identities are given in the short explanation of the painting written by Anna May (presumably with later additions from Hauschka) when it was on display in the Crystal Palace in 1918. However the pamphlet does not fully clarify just which character in this scene corresponds to which historical person, so I have endeavoured to identify the characters depicted here, see illustration 23. But firstly we need to note that the viewer gets the impression of twelve people being gathered around the sarcophagus, reflecting what was stated in the lecture extract above. This number suggests a zodiacal influence, and with the youth, this becomes the thirteen. Although Rudolf Steiner in his lecture does not mention the zodiac as such, this arrangement is described in other lectures, as a kind of archetypal template: it occurs with the twelve disciples of Christ together with Christ himself as the thirteenth. This pattern is found also with King Arthur and his twelve knights. Such patterns are always zodiacal; the extra person being a kind of higher reality that had brought the twelve and is sustaining them.

However in this painting, there is a thirteenth person in this group around the youth, although the thirteenth is almost totally obscured. Why this is the case here, is unknown. Firstly, in the background, forming an arc of a pale blue colour, are the seven Rishis; the great teachers from the Primal Indian Epoch. Rudolf Steiner taught that these seven men were reincarnated in the 13th century in central Europe, in order to participate in this momentous event.[111] So starting on the left, we have Joan of Arc, who is identifiable here as a woman holding her battle standard; on this flag there is probably an image of Jesus Christ, but the image is too unclear to be definite about this. As Anna May reports, she is here as the representative of the fifth Post-Atlantean Age. Standing next to her, tall and strong, is probably Zarathustra, representative of the second Post-Atlantean Age. Then the seven Rishis, representatives of the first Post-Atlantean Age. Then, after the seventh of the Rishis, is placed Hermes, the high initiate who is responsible for the Great Pyramid, and the associated remarkable cultural blossoming of the third Post-Atlantean Age.

The pamphlet states that the fourth Post-Atlantean Age is represented here by three people: Socrates, Plato and Augustine of Hippo. The person dressed in what appears to be white robes is Augustine, as monks in the Augustinian Order wore white robes. Then, there is the thirteenth person, almost fully obscured, whom we can assume is Socrates, and then moving further towards the right-hand side, next to Socrates must be Plato, because this man is holding the Greek 'Kerykeion' staff. This is the staff which was actually held by any highly notable Athenian: someone who was regarded as a worthy cultural ambassador for the Athenian state (or such a person could be depicted in artworks with this staff). The fourth Post-Atlantean Age is called 'the Greco-Latin Age', and Plato is a very appropriate representative of the Greek civilization, whilst Augustine is a leading figure of the Latin culture, of Roman Christianity. That Socrates is also representing the Greco-Latin Age, and is a 13th person, is enigmatic.

It is also intriguing that Joan of Arc is the representative of our current, fifth Post-Atlantean Age. The decision to choose her becomes understandable once we know that Rudolf Steiner taught that, because she was born at the end of the Holy Nights, or the Yuletide (6th Jan. 1412), she was more able to receive spiritual guidance. With this gift, she was able to take up a task given to her from the spiritual world, in particular from Archangel Michael. Her task was to oppose the aggression of the English, who at that time were seeking to dominate France. These actions opposed the intention of the higher beings, namely that the two countries should be separated from each other.[112]

---

[111] GA131, lect. 27th Jan. 1912.
[112] GA 126, lect. 28th Dec 1910, & GA 157 p. 82.

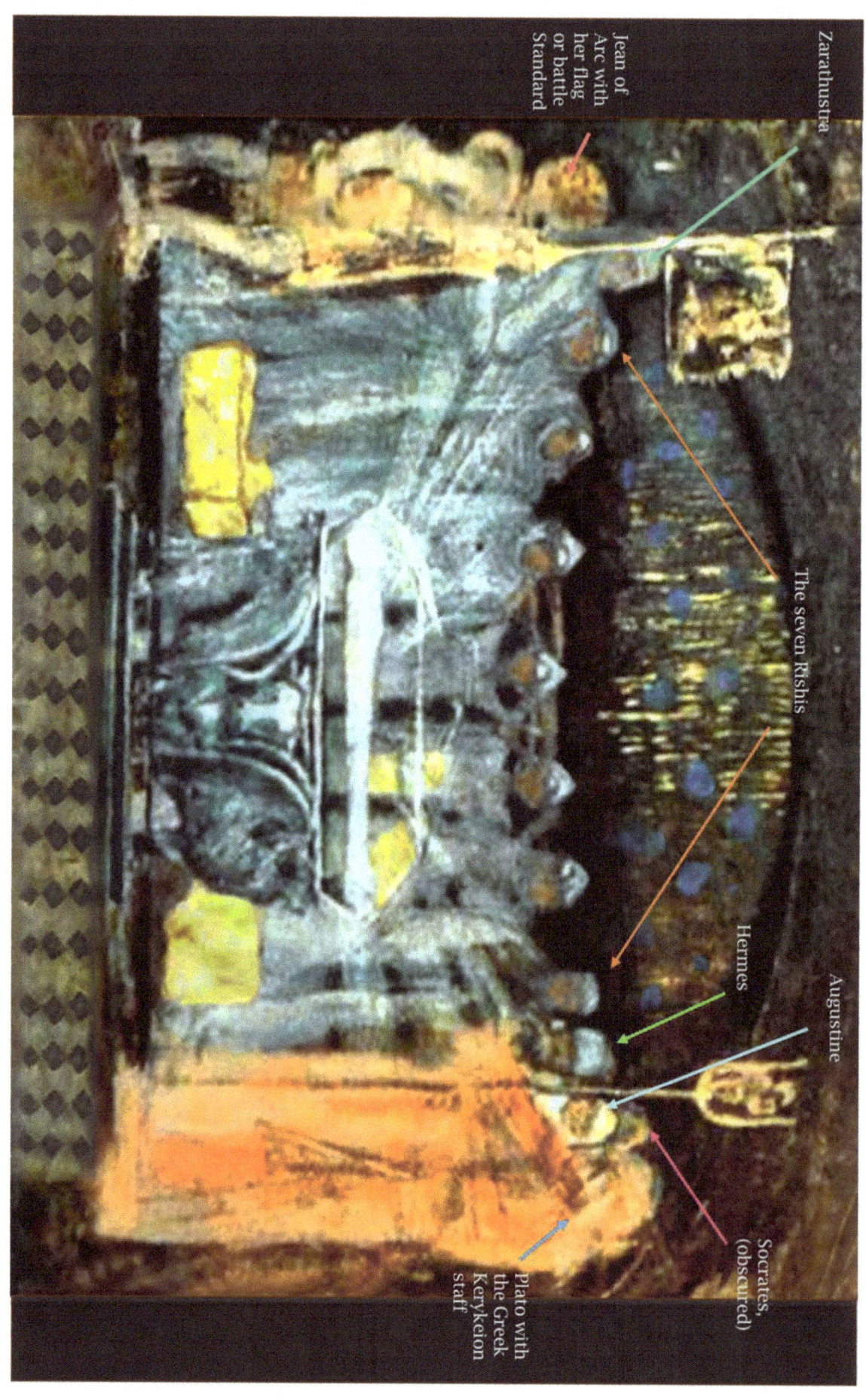

23 The various persons gathered around the sarcophagus.

# The Lower Right Side

## On the road to Damascus: The Holy of Holies

In our contemplation of this, the greatest esoteric painting Rudolf Steiner ever brought about, we have come to the holiest reality to which anthroposophy can provide insights into. This is the relationship of the human soul to Christ, and this includes the theme which Rudolf Steiner refers to as "the Reappearing of Christ". This part of the painting is directly below the scene depicting the initiation of the youth, in AD 1250. Here we see St. Paul at that moment on his journey to Damascus, when Christ Jesus makes himself visible to him. A meditative engagement with this part of the painting leads one to the theme of how does a human being encounter Christ, and this leads to some profoundly sacred words of Rudolf Steiner, not yet published, about this topic. The reason for this question arising is that, very significantly St. Paul is not depicted as gazing at the risen Jesus; instead we see, as viewers, something else. We see the flaming menorah-bush of the first part of the painting, now metamorphosed into seven roses on a bush. So we realize that the scene involving St. Paul, needs to be contemplated together with the mirror-image of the St. Paul scene in the opposite side of the painting: the experience of Moses before the burning bush, which we explored earlier.

## The Ascending dove

But before we do this, we need to become clear about two very significant highly esoteric features which I discovered in the painting, whilst working to refresh the image. Above the head of St. Paul there is a white dove; and in addition, somewhat higher up, and upside down, is the head of a bovine; see illustration 24. Why are they there? Considering firstly the dove, we discover the reason for this from a unique revelation made by Rudolf Steiner when he was commenting on the Baptism in the Jordan. We noted earlier that above the initiation scene of AD1250, there is a white dove as a symbol of the Holy Spirit, as the gospels mention; and as one would expect, this dove is descending. A dove is mentioned in the account of the baptism of Jesus by St. John, but a hidden initiatory message is contained in this. This is how it is presented in the Gospel of St. Matthew, in the NIV version,

> Mt 3:16 As soon as Jesus was baptized, he went up out of the water. At that moment, Heaven was opened, and he saw the Spirit of God descending like a dove and lighting on him. And a voice from heaven said, "This is my Son, whom I love; with him I am well pleased."

Descriptions of this event are found in the Gospel of St. Luke and of St. Mark, and they appear to be quite similar; reporting that a spiritual reality, in a dove-like form, descended down from 'heaven'. But in his commentary on the perspective within the Gospel of St. John, Rudolf Steiner, whilst affirming that indeed the Divine came upon Jesus at the Baptism, explains that, uniquely, the mention of a dove in this Johannine account refers not to a Divine **descending**, but to a high human spirituality **ascending**, "...in the form of a white dove...*a spiritual element appears, as it releases itself from the physical* {and rises up} !"[113] That is, Rudolf Steiner is teaching here that some high devachanic-astral energies were released from within the aura enveloping the physical, bodily aspect of Jesus. The account in St. John's Gospel (1:32), in the NIV version is,

> Jn 1:32 Then John gave this testimony: "I saw the Spirit come down from heaven as a dove and remain on him.
> Jn 1:33 I would not have known him, except that the One who sent me to baptize with water told me, 'The man on whom you see the Spirit come down and remain, is he who will baptize with the Holy Spirit.'
> Jn 1:34 I have seen and I testify that this is the Son of God."

This version harmonizes with the accounts in the other three Gospels, and so Rudolf Steiner's view would appear to the scholar in the Greek New Testament as improbable, and translators over the centuries have always viewed this account as referring to a divine reality descending.

---

[113] GA 112, The Gospel of St. John lecture cycle, lecture of 3rd July, 1909.

**24 The Dove & the Bull** above St. Paul.

Above: turned on an angle for clarity.

Below: the two forms above St. Paul, as in the painting.

But a meditative engagement with the original Greek text here reveals that Rudolf Steiner's view can be fully validated. For John does not mention that "the heavens opened up" (a phrase which allows the Divine to come out, and descend to the Earth). Secondly the verb for seeing used by St. John, "I saw the Spirit..." (theaomai, Θεάομαι), actually has two meanings; and while one is 'to see physically', the other meaning is 'to see clairvoyantly'. Whereas in the Gospels of Matthew and Mark, a verb for normal physical seeing only is used. Thirdly, the verb used for 'descending', whilst it does mean to descend, and is so used in the other gospel accounts, also has a second, quite special meaning. This meaning is "to gradually attain {to something}". So St. John's text can be translated not only as above:

> Then John gave this testimony: "I saw the Spirit come down from heaven as a dove and remain on him".

But also, and more accurately, like this:

> I clairvoyantly beheld the spirit, from out of the spirit {of Jesus' own being}, gradually taking on a dove-like shape, and this remained, {hovering} above him.

In other words, St. John is recording here, for those who can contemplate the Greek text with esoteric knowledge or initiatory awareness, that the finest soul-spirit aspects of Jesus rose up out of his aura, and hovered above him, forming into a chalice for the Divine that was seeking to permeate Him. It is very significant that this same dynamic is portrayed here, in regard to St. Paul encountering the risen Saviour. We shall consider this again, below. But now we need to note that before this arising of the dove occurs, a bovine force has left St. Paul, and having gone further up, is moving away from the saint. What does this second feature signify?

**The Subdued Bull forces**
We noted earlier how Taurean forces brought about the earthly ego-sense, and how this is a two-edged sword. Taurean forces long ago, were responsible for the encouraging in humanity of an earth-bound consciousness, without which human beings could not have developed a sense of "I". Rudolf Steiner describes this earthly consciousness as, "*...a thinking which only wants to understand, see, and recognize, {only} matter*", that is the material world. When he revealed processes occurring on the Earth in the Lemurian Age, which brought the human being ever further down into a material consciousness, he explained how, as the skeleton became more mineralized, human consciousness became ever more earth-bound.

> The {earthly} intelligence, the '{earthly-}word-signifying', pushed the ash, formed by the {Lemurian} volcanic fire, into this living {gelatinous} substance...and to the degree that the skeletal system condensed, the human being became ever more permeated by {earthly conceptual} thoughts, and thus by self-consciousness.[114]

To overcome the Taurean influence in one's thinking is to overcome the earthly consciousness state, which is in effect a subtly ahrimanic way of thinking, quite natural to the modern era. But in addition to this, the forces of Taurus are responsible, in regard to the sentient-soul or emotional life, for sensual desires, and these also bind a person to the Earth. The bull is well-known for its association with sensuality; it is for this reason that the lofty Mithraic cult had the {symbolic} slaying of a bull as one of its central motifs. To have a skeletal bovine face surging up and away from the spiritual seeker, is a very effective way of presenting these truths. Another way to grasp the dynamics that the acolyte on the path to esoteric Christ-centred initiation is undergoing, is to contemplate a potent esoteric depiction of this same process from ancient Egypt.

---

[114] GA 102 p. 94. In the German, „Der Sinn, {nämlich} die Wortbedeutung drängt die, sich im Verbrennungsprozeß bildende Asche, hinein in diese lebendige Substanz...und in dem Maße wie die Knochensystem verdichtete, wurde der Mensch immer mehr von Gedanken, von Selbstbewußtsein durchdrungen."

## The Heruben Papyrus

The Heruben papyrus, which was created about 1,000 BC for the tomb of a high-ranking Egyptian woman, Herytwebkit, is about her existence after death. In particular about how she undergoes soul purification in the astral realm and is then allowed to behold the mystery of eternal life. In it, in scene three, there is a remarkably esoteric painting, very relevant to the bovine head in the Anna May painting; see illustration 25. The various 'Books of the Dead' from ancient Egypt, are about what the soul and spirit undergoes in spirit realms after death; but this is the same process, in general terms, as that of being initiated.[115] Since acolytes in the ancient Egyptian Mysteries were seeking to become spiritually re-born through receiving their higher self with the help of the high sun god, or what we call today the cosmic Christ, their path has important similarities to the modern esoteric Christian path. This potent truth was directly taught by Rudolf Steiner,

> We can see in the Christian myths of the earliest times, the origin of these myths from Egyptian {initiatory} symbols... the old Egyptian teachings transformed into Christian teachings...[116]

So what does this papyrus painting reveal? Firstly, to the left, not shown in the picture, is a baboon depicted in a virile position; the reason for this is that these animals chatter as the sun rises, so they represent both reverence of the sun, and the sun as the source of creative power. Central to the image is the reddish coloured round disk of the spiritual sun, inside of which is Horus, 'the son of the (sun-)God'. Horus can be seen as a representative of the sun god, but also as the higher self of a human being. The painting is focussed on spiritual re-birth, which was central to the Egyptian understanding of life after death, and also applies to initiation. The implication here is that a human being receives their spiritual re-birth through being enveloped by sacred spiritual forces from the great sun-god, Ra (Christ). Here we see Horus holding a flail, which is an object only held by Pharaoh; this is indicating the high spiritual state of the Spiritual-self.[117]

Horus can also be depicted as being born from a lotus flower; a ritual text illustrates this, "Hail to thee, boy from the womb, child who ascends in the lotus flower, beautiful youth who comes from the Land of Light and illumines the Two Lands (Egypt) with his light..."[118]

The other features of this image represent the re-birth process. There are two green arms enveloping the Horus-child who is within the sun. This represents Horus being blessed by Atum, a deity more primeval than the sun god. Another text from ancient Egypt refers to this, in regard to two persons, *"Hail to you Atum, hail to you, Khepri {sun god}...you placed your arms around their heads, as in the "Kha" gesture, so that You might exist with your Kha in them..."*[119]

Normally, the 'Kha' in ancient Egyptian literature represents our etheric body, together with some astrality (the sentient-soul); but since the gods also possess a 'Kha', they would have this in a higher form. Below, upholding and nurturing this spiritual re-birth are the Akeru lions. They are a symbol of influences from the sun god, which are active in the earthly sphere, and hence they can also be active also in human consciousness. So we are being told that subtle influences from the sun god are making possible this birth of the Spiritual-self. And near to Horus is placed the Eye of Horus.

---

[115] Published in, A. Piankoff, *Mythological Papyri*, Princeton Univ. Press, NY Pantheon Books, 1957.
[116] Archive lecture, 8th Mar. 1902.
[117] The hieroglyphics near the sun disk are about the over-all complex journey after death and state, "Adoration of Re. The new year of Re, in the barge of Re in the sky."
[118] A Hymn, from Papyrus 3002 Berlin; in *Egyptian Solar Religion in the New Kingdom...*, Jan Assmann. RKP, 1995)
[119] *The King as God and God as King" Colour. Light and Transformation in Egyptian Ritual*, Katja Goebs, Symposium on Egyptian Royal Ideology Seminar 16-17 July 2007 2011, Harrassowitz Vlg.,Wiesbaden.

**25 Spiritual re-birth through the Sun god,** as depicted in an ancient Egyptian papyrus, and the bull forces subdued.

This symbol features in ancient Egyptian literature whenever the theme is the dramatic removal of divine (solar) forces from the earthly world (especially from a human being's consciousness) by ahrimanic forces (Seth), and therefore the need for this missing spiritual presence to be restored. The primary goal of the spiritual quest was to restore to the soul the spiritual consciousness derived from the sun-god, which this eye symbolizes. Finally, underneath the spiritual sun, in a subdued disempowered position, is a skeletal bovine face: the symbol of Taurus. This face has a very similar quality to that drawn in the Anna May painting, which serves a similar purpose.

In the Anna May painting there are some of the features which are similar to features in this significant ancient Egyptian artwork. There is the Ouroboros serpent surrounding the sun-disk, similar to that above the Tree of Life. There is also the bovine face surging up and away from Saul (who is to soon become St. Paul). He is facing Christ Jesus who represents the sun god Christ in the earthly sphere; and the blessing of the Father-god (Atum) is implied here, since the Saviour is the portal to Him. The Eye of Horus, as a symbol of (re-achieving) spiritual consciousness, could be thought of as represented by the seven roses, which are about a spiritualizing of the 'fallen' earthly consciousness.

### St. Paul encounters the Risen Christ

In the first section of the painting, we saw three people standing near the entrance to the Holy of Holies in Solomon's temple; and below this, the seven-branched menorah indicating the cosmic origin of the human being, sustained by Jahve-Christ, which exists hidden within the soul. Over in this right-hand section, we are seeing the counterpart to this, but just what is this sacred mystery? We see Saul, on the road to Damascus, suddenly beholding the Saviour, in the ethers. But the viewer, looking beyond the awed and astonished Saul, is not shown the risen Christ Jesus. What do we see instead? It is here in this painting that we encounter an especially holy mystery. The seven flames of the menorah, in front of Moses, have become seven roses; the central rose is surrounded by a crown of thorns, from which rays of spiritual light stream forth. A kind of bush with seven roses is alluding to the well-known rose-cross symbol, which was created by Lazaros-John, in his medieval incarnation as Christian Rosencreutz.

We recall that this painting is depicting the Christ Mystery in relation to the mission of Christian Rosencreutz, as unfolding over several lifetimes, and thus the Rosicrucian movement, also. It is from this perspective that the relationship of the human being to Christ Jesus is being depicted here. Instead of an image of the Saviour in an etheric form, we are being shown something else. A sentence from an ancient Manichaean psalm is helpful to begin our contemplation; "*He is the leader on the Path, and He is the treasure which we are seeking.*"[120] These words are embodied in the following famous passage in the Gospels from Christ, as he answers a question from St. Thomas,

> Jesus answered, "I am the way and the truth and the life." (John 14:6) [121]

These Greek words include the expression "ego eimi" (ἐγώ εἰμι) which is literally, "I, I am" or in its esoteric meaning, "the I, I am". So these words in the Greek language, contemplated with esoteric awareness, reveals that Christ is declaring this,

> "The sense of 'I' which has I myself (Christ) within it, **is** the way, the truth and the life."

In the light of anthroposophy, one can conclude that 'The Way' is the Spirit-human or Atman, and 'The Truth' is the Spiritual-self, and so 'The Life' refers to the Life-Spirit. These three constitute the human being's eternal self or higher self. It is these words, amongst many others, which reveal the deeply esoteric sacredness of the Gospels, for here Christ Jesus is saying that he **is** the "I am" (the I-sense in human beings).

---

[120] From *Manichaean Psalm Book*, Edit. C. Allberry, Kohlhammer Vlg, Stuttgart, 1938.
[121] In the Greek, λέγει αὐτῷ [ὁ] Ἰησοῦς· ἐγώ εἰμι ἡ ὁδὸς καὶ ἡ ἀλήθεια καὶ ἡ ζωή· οὐδεὶς ἔρχεται πρὸς τὸν πατέρα εἰ μὴ δι᾽ ἐμοῦ.

**The new Holy of Holies within: the Saviour and the eternal "I am"**
But to contemplate with deeper understanding this section of the painting, we need now to add further words about the relationship of the Christ to the human being, from that deep initiatory book, the Book of the Apocalypse, by St. John. This book, as with the Gospel of St. John, was written by Lazaros-John, whom we now refer to as Christian Rosencreutz, so the Anna May painting can certainly be expected to have features which allude to the teachings of these books,

> These are the words of him who holds the seven stars in his right hand and walks among the seven golden lampstands. (Rev. 2:1)

These seven stars, although ambiguous in the Greek, are, as Rudolf Steiner made clear, the seven planets of our solar system; from these our astral body is formed. Christ is presented in the Apocalypse as a macrocosmic (or planetary) human being, As Rudolf Steiner taught in regard to the Apocalypse,

> Christ encompasses all seven {planets}...the seven planets are related to him as the limbs of the body, to the body as a whole.[122]

From the highest astral planetary influences, the seven chakras form, when the astral body is purified. The chakras are referred to as lotus flowers in the Orient, and are represented by the roses in the Rosicrucian stream. The rose-cross symbol is a meditative image which speaks of how, through the sacrificial deed of Christ on the cross, the human being can find the spiritual capacity to transform their astral body, until it becomes a beautiful, radiant aura glittering with the splendor of the developed seven chakras.

The roses symbolize the purity of the soul in a meditant who has worked successfully towards spirituality. That there are seven of these roses indicates that the seven chakras are developing. One experiences a feeling of holiness when doing this meditation earnestly, as many deep truths are contained within it. The cross shape is vital, for it indicates to the meditant, for example, that it is through the power of the cosmic sun-god that spiritual development is now possible for humanity. The union of this being, whom Steiner referred to as the being of love, to the soul of the Earth has opened up this possibility. It is this being which was also revered in the highest mystery centre of ancient Atlantis: the Sun Mysteries.

The cross shape proclaims that the cosmic sun-god Christ, is the source of the meditant's inner ability to overcome the lower self; and this being could also be called the Spirit of the Earth, now that It is united to the soul of the Earth. This same cross shape is also indicating that our capacity to develop to a spiritual state of consciousness derives from this same divine source of light.

So, whereas St. Paul saw the etheric Risen Jesus, the viewer of this painting sees the transformation of the sevenfold menorah-bush of Moses, into a bush with seven roses. That is, we are beholding the sevenfold soul-forces, but now sanctified; the seven roses represent the seven chakras which 'blossom' when the astral body has become ennobled, bringing into birth the higher self; see illustration 26. But, since this image here is in effect a replacement for the Risen Saviour, we are also being told two things:

- This radiant sevenfold higher self is the Saviour Himself, in a certain sense; and that,
- This higher self has its origin in the spiritual light from the Saviour, a light which derives from the light of the cosmic Christ permeating the Earth.

The viewer is also being told that this spiritualization is a process made possible by Jesus – by his sacrifice, which is signified by the crown of thorns placed around the heart chakra. The painting points to the presence of Christ Jesus in the heart of the initiated person – but as a process for which the sacrifices and striving of Christian Rosencreutz have been bringing about crucial support. This is the result of his striving, during his life as Hiram in the time of Solomon,

---

[122] GA 104a, lect. 22nd April 1907.

then through to his life in the first century, as Lazaros, as he became Lazaros-John, when he was resurrected by Jesus, in a process which resembled the ancient initiation process, but also heralded its demise. Then, Lazaros-John in a medieval life underwent the initiation which the Anna May painting depicts, which led to the creation of the Rosicrucian movement.

**The nature of Jesus Christ in anthroposophy**
To really understand this section of the painting, we remind ourselves that it is a core truth in anthroposophy that, at the Baptism in the Jordan, Jesus became united to the cosmic Christ, becoming Jesus Christ. To counter some views about the nature of Jesus Christ, which I regard as incorrect to Rudolf Steiner's teachings, we need to achieve a clear understanding here. This sublime process was fully consolidated at the Resurrection, which occurred on April 5th, AD 33. Through this, Jesus became the crucially important archetype of the spiritually re-born human being: the human being who has achieved their eternal higher ego. For once such an archetype has been created, then all human beings, who so will, can become spiritually re-born in the course of time.

**The World Saviour**
Once this Baptism took place, there occurred the union of the soul and spirit of Jesus, (whose birth is recorded in St. Luke's Gospel, and whose ancestor was Nathan the priest), to the cosmic Christ: a situation which became an eternal reality as from the Resurrection. From that day on (April 5th AD 33), the 'Nathan-Jesus' soul, as such, disappears from the world, because he became 'Jesus Christ'. That is, he is a divine person, in whose self or "I", is the cosmic Christ; for, as Rudolf Steiner taught, Jesus Christ is the archetype of the future, fully perfected human being: that is a human being with the Spirit-self, the Life-spirit and the Spirit-human. [123] We know from Rudolf Steiner's lectures on the Gospels, that this person is the unique, and uniquely divine, unfallen soul who had his first, and only, incarnation in Palestine, and who then became the vessel of the cosmic Christ. Rudolf Steiner taught that this divine soul has, "all the love {capacity} that a human being can ever attain".[124]

We have seen that the bush of seven roses represents the higher self of the human being, and yet it also represents Christ Jesus. To understand this, we need to know that Rudolf Steiner revealed that the soul and spirit qualities of the Saviour exist as what one could call 'replicas'. These radiant, spiritual forms or 'divine energies' from Christ Jesus, embodying the qualities of the Saviour, are bestowed upon truly spiritual souls. So one can say, in very inadequate earthly language, there exist 'copies' of the feeling-life (or sentient-soul), and the understanding (or intellectual-soul) and the intuitive awareness (or spiritual-soul) of Christ Jesus. Rudolf Steiner reports that some of these have been bestowed upon a number of great Christian persons in history. For example, in the aura of St. Francis of Assisi there was a replica of the sentient-soul of the Saviour.

But, extremely significantly, Rudolf Steiner also revealed that there exist replicas of the ego or divine, yet human, "I" of Jesus Christ. Rudolf Steiner revealed the deeply sacred, intimate soul-truth that, at the Resurrection, countless replicas of the "I" of Jesus Christ were created, and that those human beings who so will to evolve themselves up to the Spirit-self, can absorb one of these 'replicas' into their own core self, into their higher ego-sense – as it becomes the Spirit-self or devachanic aura.

---

[123] In the books of Sergei Prokofieff, the name "Jesus" usually means the "Nathan Jesus soul". His use of the term 'Christ', though extensive, is misleading, as he often means the cosmic Christ. But if he is referring to "Jesus", it is the 'Nathan Jesus' soul; i.e., the still-existing, unchanged 'Nathan Jesus' soul, an ego-less vessel of a deity. His assertions that Jesus (-Christ) "is principally an etheric being" is deeply incorrect and very misleading; e.g., "The cycle of the year as a path of initiation to experience the Christ" p. 343).
[124] GA 142, *The Bhagavad Gita and the Epistles of St. Paul*, lecture, 9th Jan. 1913.

26 **The new Holy of Holies** St. Paul experiences the risen Jesus, but we see the macrocosmic human, with planetary forces made noble and the zodiac's influences becoming transformed also.

**The Holy Grail**
This theme brings us directly to another especially sacred truth, which also is linked to the theme of the Holy Grail. We have seen that the Holy Grail is depicted in the left and the central sections of the triptych; now we discover that it is also present, in its most profound sense, in the right section of this painting, but in a veiled way. For, in an especially sacred moment during his lecture work in 1909, Rudolf Steiner revealed more about this remarkable process of the multiplying of astral-devachanic 'forms', which are copies of the actual divine 'ego-sense' which our Saviour has, as the bearer of the archetype of the threefold eternal ego.

He revealed, in words so inspired that they are difficult to transfer into written form, that this holy reality, of replicas of the Saviour's 'ego', is what constitutes the mystery of the Holy Grail,

> The Brotherhood of the Holy Grail guarded this secret of the replicas of the Ego of Jesus Christ. Today the time has arrived, where these secrets may be proclaimed, if the hearts of people make themselves {sufficiently} mature through a spiritual {way of} life, so that they are able to raise themselves to the understanding of this great Mystery; that is, if these souls allow themselves, through Spiritual Science, to be enflamed to understanding of such secrets. That is to say, if our souls live into such an understanding, then in this way, the soul shall become sufficiently mature, through gazing at this holy chalice, to come to know the Mystery of the Christ-Ego, the Mystery of the Eternal Ego, which every human ego can become.
>
> ***There*** it is, this secret – however, people need to allow themselves to be summoned through Spiritual Science, to understand this secret **as a reality**, in order to receive the Christ-Ego, through gazing at the Holy Grail {as an Idea}. To do this, one has to **understand** what has occurred {at the Resurrection} **as a reality,** to view this **as a reality**, {this creating of replicas of the "I" of Christ Jesus }. And then, if people become ever more prepared for the reception of the Christ-I, then shall the Christ-I ever more pour itself into the souls of people.[125] People shall then evolve themselves up to where their great archetype, Christ Jesus, is. Then people shall begin to learn to understand to what degree Christ Jesus is the great prototype of {the future redeemed} humanity...[126] (transl. AA)

In that same year when Rudolf Steiner revealed these profound truths about the Grail, he spoke of this theme quite directly, in the land where the archangel Vidar is especially present (i.e., Norway).[127] This is the archangel from whom derives the deepest presentation of the Grail in all the legends created about the Grail. Rudolf Steiner told his listeners,

> In that people absorb anthroposophy, they take up a kind of copy of the ego of Christ Jesus {into themselves}.[128]

This extraordinarily significant statement is embodied in this painting. So what was, 2,000 years ago, the 'ego' of the 'Nathan Jesus soul'? In so far as this divine person had never incarnated until his lifetime in Palestine, Jesus did not have what Rudolf Steiner calls the {normal} "ahrimanic-luciferic ego" of human beings. This kind of ego developed in human beings over long ages of incarnating under the influence of fallen spirit powers. However, without some sense of self, the young Jesus would have had no capacity to function in the world at all. So he would have naturally developed his own, if delicate, earthly sense of self; and this was strengthened, as Rudolf Steiner taught, by the proximity of his friend and cousin, John the Baptist, and later, especially by the great sage Zarathustra, who was also a childhood friend.

However, just before the Baptism in the Jordan, the external support of his ego-sense provided by the sage Zarathustra left him; but Jesus within minutes of this happening, walked towards the

---

[125] In the light of such revelations, the view that Christ Jesus is still the 'Nathan Jesus' and is also "mainly composed of etheric energy", is again shown to be disturbingly incorrect.
[126] GA 109, lect. 11th April, 1909.
[127] To learn more about this Archangel as the inspirer of anthroposophy, see the author's book, "*The Vidar Flame Column - its meaning from Rudolf Steiner*".
[128] GA 104a, p.104.

River Jordan where John the Baptist was baptizing people. Jesus then became united to the descending cosmic Christ: that great Sun-god from whom the Spirit-self, the Life-spirit and the Spirit-human all derive.[129] These three strands of the human spirit create the higher "I"; this is the eternal ego. So Jesus Christ then became the most empowered and divine of all human beings, with an 'ego-sense' which is the most sublime and powerful that it is possible to have. In the words of Rudolf Steiner,

> ...although a cosmic principle lives in him, Christ Jesus as an individual personality confronts other human beings quite individually..."[130]

**The Etheric Reappearing of Christ Jesus**
My readers are probably aware of the teachings of Rudolf Steiner in regard to this special theme. In essence, it concerns what in the Christian world is called "the Second Coming of Christ". This concerns the dawning of a delicate etheric clairvoyance in humanity, as of about the year 1900. In response to this new capacity of humanity, the Saviour has undertaken to enshroud himself in an etheric form, so as to make himself visible to people. However Rudolf Steiner also explained that this process has been substantially assisted by the immense spiritual greatness of Christian Rosencreutz,

> By the grace of what radiated from the wonderful etheric body of Christian Rosencreutz, the Rosicrucians could develop an absolutely new world conception. What has been developed by the Rosicrucians up to our time is work of both an outer and an inner nature. The outer work was for the purpose of discovering what lies behind the 'Maya' of the material world. They wanted to investigate the 'Maya' of matter. Just as man has an etheric body, so does the whole of the macrocosm have an etheric macrocosm, an etheric body. There is a certain point of transition from the coarser to the finer substance. Let us look at the boundary between physical and etheric substance. What lies between physical and etheric substance is like nothing else in the world. It is neither gold nor silver, lead nor copper. It is something that cannot be compared with any other physical substance, yet it is the essence of all of them.

> It is a substance that is contained in every other physical substance, so that the other physical substances can be considered to be modifications of this one substance. To see this substance clairvoyantly was the endeavour of the Rosicrucians. The preparation, the development of such vision, they knew required a heightened activity of the soul's moral forces, which would then enable them to see this substance. They realised that the power for this vision lay in the moral power of the soul. This substance was really seen and discovered by the Rosicrucians. {This is an inner, esoteric 'alchemy'.} They found that this substance existed in the world in a certain form, both in the macrocosm and in man. In the world outside the human being, they revered it as the mighty garment of the macrocosm. They saw it arising in man when there is a harmonious interplay between thinking and willing. They saw the Will-forces as being not only in man, but in the macrocosm also, for instance in thunder and lightning. And they saw the forces of thought on the one hand in man, and also outside in the world, in the rainbow and the rosy light of dawn. The Rosicrucians sought the strength to achieve such harmony of willing and thinking in their own soul in the force radiating from this etheric body of the thirteenth, Christian Rosencreutz.

> Thus the forces radiating from the etheric body of Christian Rosencreutz continued to be active in the nineteenth century, too. And a renewal of theosophical life could come about

---

[129] It was for me a special experience, in 1979, to open one of Rudolf Steiner's 600 notebooks, and read in his own hand-writing, the notes of this same event, written down shortly after he had seen this himself, in the Akashic Record.

[130] GA 139, *The Gospel of St. Mark*, 17th Sept. 1909, lecture 3. Although Steiner reported that, as the cosmic Christ descended, the enhancement of his ego-sense which had been especially arranged to help Jesus, went away, his own delicate earthly ego (and soul) was nevertheless the vessel into which the true higher, eternal ego came. The departure of the 'ego' refers to Zarathustra's powerful ego that was assisting Jesus from his 12th to his 30th year of life.

because by 1899 the little Kali Yuga had run its course {There is also a large Kali Yuga Age}. That is why the approach to the spiritual world is easier now and spiritual influence is possible to a far greater degree. The etheric body of Christian Rosencreutz has become very strong, and, through devotion to this, man will be able to acquire the new clairvoyance; and lofty spiritual forces will come into being. This will only be possible, however, for those people who follow the training of Christian Rosencreutz correctly.

Until now an esoteric Rosicrucian preparation was essential, but the twentieth century has the mission of enabling this etheric body to become so powerful that it can also work exoterically. Those affected by it will be granted the experience of the event that Paul experienced on the road to Damascus. Until now this etheric body has only worked into the school of the Rosicrucians; in the twentieth century more and more people will be able to experience the effect of it, and through this they will come to experience the appearance of Christ in the etheric body. It is the work of the Rosicrucians that makes possible the etheric vision of Christ. The number of people who will become capable of seeing it will grow and grow. We must attribute this re-appearance to the important work of the {group of} twelve people and the thirteenth, in the thirteenth and fourteenth centuries. (Lecture: The Rosicrucian Christianity; 27th Sept. 1911: GA 130)

It is important to remind ourselves here that, by the expression "true Rosicrucianism", Rudolf Steiner means anthroposophical wisdom, not the teachings spread by the various 'Rosicrucian' societies still existing today.

**The revelation from Rudolf Steiner about the response of Christ Jesus to being tormented and crucified**

In the Steiner Archives is located a priceless document, identified as notes of lecture given in 1910, in Stockholm, about the Reappearing of Jesus in the ethers. A full transcript was not made of this special talk, but the sacred core of it was noted down.[129] The lecture is about the gifts of Christ Jesus to human beings, which assist the spiritual renewal of humanity; that is the inner spiritual awakening that occurs as a result of the Reappearing of Jesus in the ethers; the so-called Second Coming. These acts of Grace are revealed as his response to being tormented and crucified, long ago on Golgotha hill. The implied spiritual dynamics which Rudolf Steiner refers to as the result of the Reappearing of Jesus, have not exerted their full impact. One reason for this, is that the proclamation of these truths, which would have awakened people to this influence from the ethers, which Rudolf Steiner forecast would happen in the 1930's, did not happen.[130] There is of course, the possibility that such spiritual influences from Christ could perhaps manifest in a later century. In any event, it is very helpful to include these deeply inspired words. These notes are brief, and include some cryptic phrases; so some comments are added in brackets, for clarity. Also the terms 'Jesus Christ' and 'Christ Jesus' interchangeably;

> Jesus Christ was wrongly judged and convicted by people. But with Christ there is no such thing as revenge, for he brings into the world the dissolving of the principle of revenge. Thus judging and convicting, from the viewpoint of Jesus Christ, means that he shall awaken the conscience of humanity upon his reappearing. He shall then have the possibility to undertake a step, which shall call forth in humanity the conscience.
> The first dawning light of the reappearing to humanity's awareness of Jesus Christ will be a radiance of elemental feelings of conscience. These feelings shall take hold of humanity's consciousness with elemental power. As a result, without people knowing from whence this comes, there shall arise in their souls feelings of shame. So, poetically

---

[129] Some small fragments of texts from Steiner, often privately shared by members, were at times thought to originate from one of his students. This text was published in a book by V. Tomberg, but I conclude that it comes Rudolf Steiner, and was given in, or privately after, the lecture in Stockholm on 12th January, 1910. Officially recorded (in the H. Schmidt *Register*) as a Members-only lecture, "The Appearance of Christ in the Etheric". The lecture report does not include this fragment, but some lecture notes are incomplete; also more esoteric sections of lectures were at times withheld from publication.

[130] It appears that this was due to the tragically premature death of Rudolf Steiner, who forecast that the Reappearing of Jesus in the ethers would be proclaimed extensively in the early 1930's; but his premature death prevented this.

one could say, the first signs of the dawn of the reappearing of Christ to humanity's consciousness shall be the reddish blush of shame.

In this way people shall experience with irresistible power their disappointment in the values which they regarded so highly, as the true and the beautiful. And thus they shall have to experience a reversal of all the values or priorities in their souls. The soul in the After-life, in Kamaloca, has to experience a reversal of all their values or priorities because they then are existing within the rays of the 'cosmic conscience'. In a similar way, so shall humanity now have to experience a reversal of all the values or priorities in life, because they shall experience the efficacy of the Christ in the spatial world. This influence of Christ shall become efficacious in space, in the horizontal dynamic.*

And if Christ Jesus' **was whipped** in the past and **crowned with thorns**, then this signifies now that he shall not only awaken the conscience of humanity but also that **he shall gently touch this conscience**. Just as he then experienced whipping, so shall he now gently touch humanity; that is, those people who experience doubt about the deeper meaning of life.

He shall gently touch their souls, so **that they may be imbued with solace and courage**. This gentle touching of the soul, to let in courage for a new creative impulse is the result of **the flogging {which he received}**. As a result, there shall be people who say, "We are starting radiantly anew, for everything that was already created cannot withstand this light." It is as if the first deed of creation from within the human realm should begin. People shall receive this courage not from out of themselves, but from the gentle touching which emanates forth from Christ.

And if he was **crowned with thorns** in the past, he shall consequently give tasks to individuals and groups of people as to how they are to serve his work. He shall **crown humanity with love-imbued duties**. There exists in the world, the idea of duty. This sense of pure duty shall sometime bring humanity into catastrophe. For everything evil that is brought into the world, people do through this sense of duty {for duty's sake}. But from Christ Jesus shall 'love-duties' be distributed, to individuals and groups of people, when the etheric Reappearing occurs. Then a colossus shall fall, for instead of duty, love-deeds shall be the task that needs to be done.

And if in the past, the Christ **had to carry his cross**, upon which he was to be crucified, thus shall the Christ as he reappears in the ether, **heal people from their afflictions** so that destiny healings can proceed from him, so that people who bear their cross, shall have the power to carry it through a soul-physical healing.

(*The expression "destiny healings" ('Schicksalsheilungen') appears to refer to situations wherein people become healed because, with help from the Saviour, the past karmic causes, or current personal errors in attitudes and mind-set, responsible for their illness, have been realized, acknowledged and balanced out.*)

And when in the past, Christ Jesus **was crucified**, whereby he proclaimed, "Father forgive them for they know not what they do", then in these words there is also contained what his Will actually is; namely in the space which is granted to him, to exert an influence, so that, as a karmic result of the Crucifixion, **people shall know what they are doing**.

(*The expression, "karmic result of the Crucifixion" refers to the new situation that the Saviour, as an act of Grace, seeks to so transform the dynamics of karma that, instead of Himself seeking to be compensated for the wrongs He suffered, He shall exert an influence in people's souls that enhances their consciousness, so that people today **become aware of the consequences of what they are doing** – especially in regard to important spiritual obligations and opportunities. This deed of the Saviour stands there, as the example of how to transform the 'eye for an eye, tooth for a tooth" dynamic of karma, into one of good-will for one's enemies. Rudolf Steiner elsewhere revealed that, as of the mid-twentieth century,*

*Christ Jesus has become the 'Lord of Karma'. That is, he is now taking up the task of helping human beings to realize what their karmic dynamics are, and how to best work with these, for the benefit of humanity.)*

The karmic result of the fact that Christ Jesus was {*bound and*} crucified shall be that, humanity is not just {*having to exist as if*} bound up, and as if crucified (in earthly life) – but that their eyes shall be opened, so that a new clairvoyance shall be aroused through Christ Jesus, **so that humanity shall know and see what they do**. A karmic clairvoyance shall arise: a seeing of karma {of karmic consequences of what we do}. When people of today do something they do not know what shall be its karmic consequence. But people of the near future shall know this; they shall know what they do. Karmic clairvoyance is the answer of the Christ to his being crucified, which happened because people did not know what they did.

Thus does the Christ transform the negative into the positive. In the etheric reappearing of the Christ, there shall be responses of these kinds, to the type of treatment which he experienced when he lived as a man amongst humanity.


**Note:**
\* The very brief expression, "the horizontal dynamic" ("Wirkung des Christus im Raume, in der Horizontal..."), is at first quite puzzling, but it becomes understandable through a section of Rudolf Steiner's *Foundation Stone Meditation*,

> ...For efficacious is the Christ-will from horizon unto horizon,
> bestowing Grace on the soul in the rhythms of the cosmos....

In the lecture Rudolf Steiner gave when he introduced this meditation he explained,

> The Christ-power which is efficacious throughout the periphery of the horizon, which weaves in and through the streams of air, circling around the Earth, and which actively has an influence within our breathing system.

As I wrote in *The Foundation Stone Meditation – a New Commentary*:
> We noted earlier that the three sections invoke a kind of world-cross. Forces from the Father-God arise up from inside the Earth, and forces from the Holy Spirit descend. Here in this middle section {of the large verse}, forces are efficacious on us **horizontally**. So, then one has to extend this idea of the over-arching firmament or periphery of the globe into the human existential sphere. From the viewpoint of a person living on the surface of the Earth, this periphery is the current horizon merging into a succession of changing horizons that curve downwards ahead of you, and to the left and the right as well, as one imagines a movement across the surface of the Earth.
>
> The expression, 'from horizon unto horizon' accurately translates the primary meaning of the word here. As Rudolf Steiner explained in lectures on art, "the human being experiences the circumference-periphery (Umkreis) of the Earth with the middle section {of one's corporeal being}; the {heart} area, with the feelings."[131] This middle section of the great verse appeals to the refining of our feelings. The ambiguous word 'feelings' has both meanings here. The emotions or desires, and also sensing with the body's sense organs of either the physical or etheric worlds.

So this expression, "the horizontal dynamic" here, is saying that humanity, if people so will, shall be experiencing inner guidance and help from Christ Jesus, but in addition to this, on a deeper level, subtle influences from the cosmic Christ, who dwells within the planet's aura. These influences shall have an effect in the emotions, as emotional uplift and insights, or as a subtle feeling-sensing, which creates a delicate 'atmosphere', like a half-remembered dream. The new

---

[131] From GA 291, "Das Wesen der Farben" Lecture, June 2nd 1923, p. 179.

festival cycle which Rudolf Steiner laid the foundation for, in his lectures on the spiritual influences active in the seasons, are intended to help people to develop a sensitivity to the Christ-influence. The experience of Jesus Christ in the ether can also be more powerful, more directly cognized; it depends upon the person and the situation.

**A report of an encounter with Christ Jesus in the ether**
Before we consider the remaining features of the painting, the reader will find it especially uplifting to know that if one searches, one can find reports of experiences that many people have had of the Saviour, appearing as if physically before them, without the person being in a religious state of mind. But in fact Jesus is in an etheric form, which appears as if physical. The person is seeing into the ethers for a short time, and Jesus Christ makes himself visible to them in an etheric form, before he withdraws. The number of people having this experience is unknown, but it will be considerable (two of my students have had this experience.)

I well remember hearing in the 1980's of a striking example of this 'reappearing' in an etheric form of Christ Jesus occurred to a small group of anthroposophists in Germany, during the Second World War. He appeared inside a closed room just after a study evening was completed, and approached each member of the astonished and awed group, briefly, intoning a very brief meditative word to each one, before moving back from them and saying to the entire group, "Remember, I am with you until the end of the Earth Age", before fading out of sight.

This encounter was more powerful because the five or six people involved, having an interest in anthroposophy, could be briefly communicated with, whereas from other reports, it is clear that normally this does not occur. The person sees him, and after a short time he fades from their view, leaving the chosen person with many questions that prompt them to consider their relation to Christ Jesus.

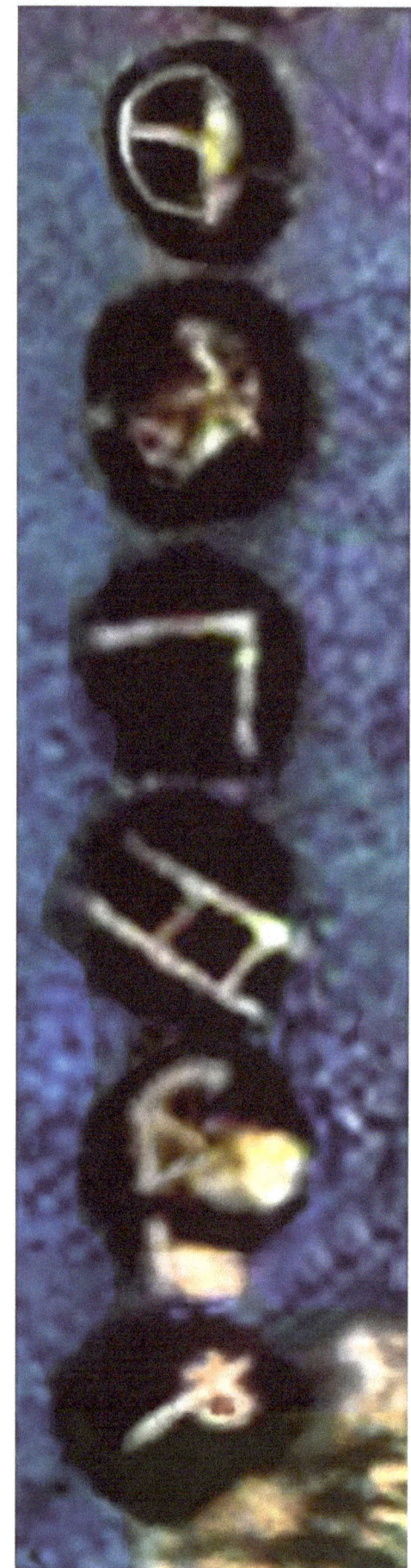

27 **The 'Masonic' zodiac:** the 12 images relate to ethical requirements of Freemasonry.

**The Zodiac beneath the bush of seven roses**
Earlier, we noted that the sevenfold menorah bush near Moses, together with the zodiac depictions underneath him represent a kind of the matrix of the human soul and earthly ego-sense. That is, the seven planets within the astral body and the twelve-fold zodiac influence, which underlies our body and our senses and part of our higher ego. But in the right side of the painting, the seven flames have become roses, so the astral influences have blossomed into noble qualities. Likewise, the zodiacal influences are to become more conscious, and more refined. Consequently, more or less traditional zodiac symbols have now been exchanged for symbols which speak of specific virtues, specific soul qualities; in particular as this is presented in Freemasonry, see illustration 27. Here are the 12 symbols used in the painting, although two of these are not clear enough to identify. The sequence goes left to right, and below is a brief note as to what they can mean in Freemasonry:

1: A key = control of speech, thus control of the heart

2: A guarding spirit being = the cherubim guarding entry to Paradise

3: A sword = justice
      Or = possibly, the renewal of the power of speech

4: Two crossed knives = truth & justice, or fraternal comradeship
      Or = the 'crucified' World-Soul of Plato

5: A ram = the Lamb of God

6: This symbol is too unclear to identify

7: This symbol is too unclear to identify

8: Possibly a bull = its meaning is unknown, except in general terms, it signifies Taurus

9: The scythe = the significance of death to the spiritual seeker

10: A ladder = the path up to the spirit worlds, as with Jacob's dream

11: The Ark with anchor = The Ark is 'hope', and the anchor is 'faith'

12: The adze or gavel = a reminder that the Freemason's soul is to be worked on, evolving up from a rough 'stone' to becoming a perfectly 'smoothed out' person


To help people work with the challenges and opportunities that the zodiac sun-signs create for us, Rudolf Steiner wrote twelve verses, which are profound meditations on the actual challenges for the soul of each sun-sign. See my *The Lost Zodiac of Rudolf Steiner*, which presents a careful translation of these, together with a commentary.

## The Fall of Lucifer

Somewhat obscured, in the far right side of the painting, there is what appears to be a depiction of Lucifer falling; see illustration 28. This does not mean the original ethical fall from the divine state of the hierarchical beings, in the Moon Aeon. This scene refers to another very significant theme in anthroposophy: the gradual redemption of Lucifer, which he at first experiences as a fall. This is a contemporary, not an ancient process: a process wherein Lucifer 'falls' from his current position of false grandeur, and self-centred arrogance, and arises as a redeemed ethical being. So this 'fall' is a weakening of his false power, which is then followed by an arising, or returning back to a divine state of being. This artistic motif was later incorporated into the great wooden sculpture designed by Rudolf Steiner, *The Group*, which is also known as *The Representative of Man*. It is also an artistic motif in earlier German religious art.

It was in the previous aeon, the Moon Aeon, that Lucifer fell, which was at the time when human beings were being given astrality by the gods: that is when they were receiving their own astral body. This interweaving of two processes resulted in the inherent presence of luciferic qualities in the primitive astrality of human beings, in the next aeon, which is now our current 'Earth' aeon. So our destiny and the future of Lucifer are intimately intertwined. Lucifer is depicted not far from the image of the future Spirit-self human being (or Sophia person), indicating that, as the Spirit-self is developed in the spiritual seeker, Lucifer loses his power over that person.

The somewhat distressed state that Lucifer is portrayed in as he 'falls', (that is, as he starts to become redeemed), is caused by human beings spiritualizing themselves, through the help of the Christ-Impulse. For this spiritualizing of the soul is experienced as a fiery torment for the luciferic spirits.[132] Furthermore, it is, as Rudolf Steiner explains, when luciferic spirits are redeemed, that Lucifer's role in human evolving really becomes a blessing, for then that human being has attained to his or her Spirit-self – he or she has 'lifted up The Son of Man'. This is a high and significant achievement, but it is one, which required as a starting point, Lucifer's fallen qualities, which triggered off a sense of self, inciting the soul to self-centred attitudes and sensual desires.

Many spirits amongst the hosts of Lucifer have already been redeemed, and it is especially through the spiritualizing of humanity that this has occurred. Consequently in our painting, this depiction of Lucifer falling down is placed near to the 'Sophia' soul, or future, redeemed human being. As human beings become Spirit-self people, Lucifer goes through a transformation.

---

[132] GA 107, lect. 22nd Mar. 1909.

## 28 The Fall of Lucifer

Above left: the Anna May depiction of a what appears to be Lucifer falling.
Above right: from the wooden statue, Lucifer falls, (obscured behind the Christ figure).

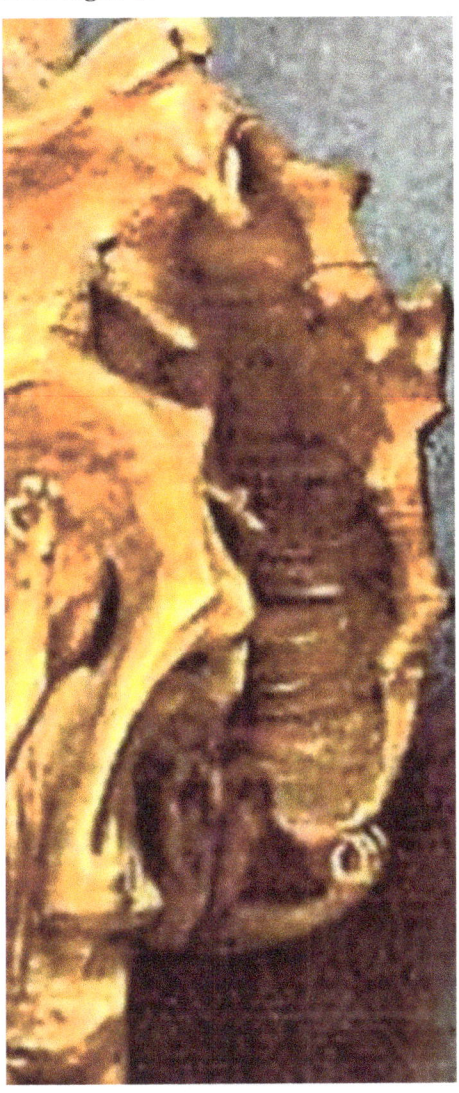

Cultural antecedents:
Below left: Simon Magus falling as an evil spirit, 1130 AD Autun Cathedral.
Below right: Dore's depiction of Lucifer falling from Milton's *Paradise Lost*.

## 29 The Sophia state of spirituality in the far future

This image is similar to that of the woman in the Apocalypse with the moon at her feet.

There is an unclear moon shape at her feet, and she has the sun in her heart.

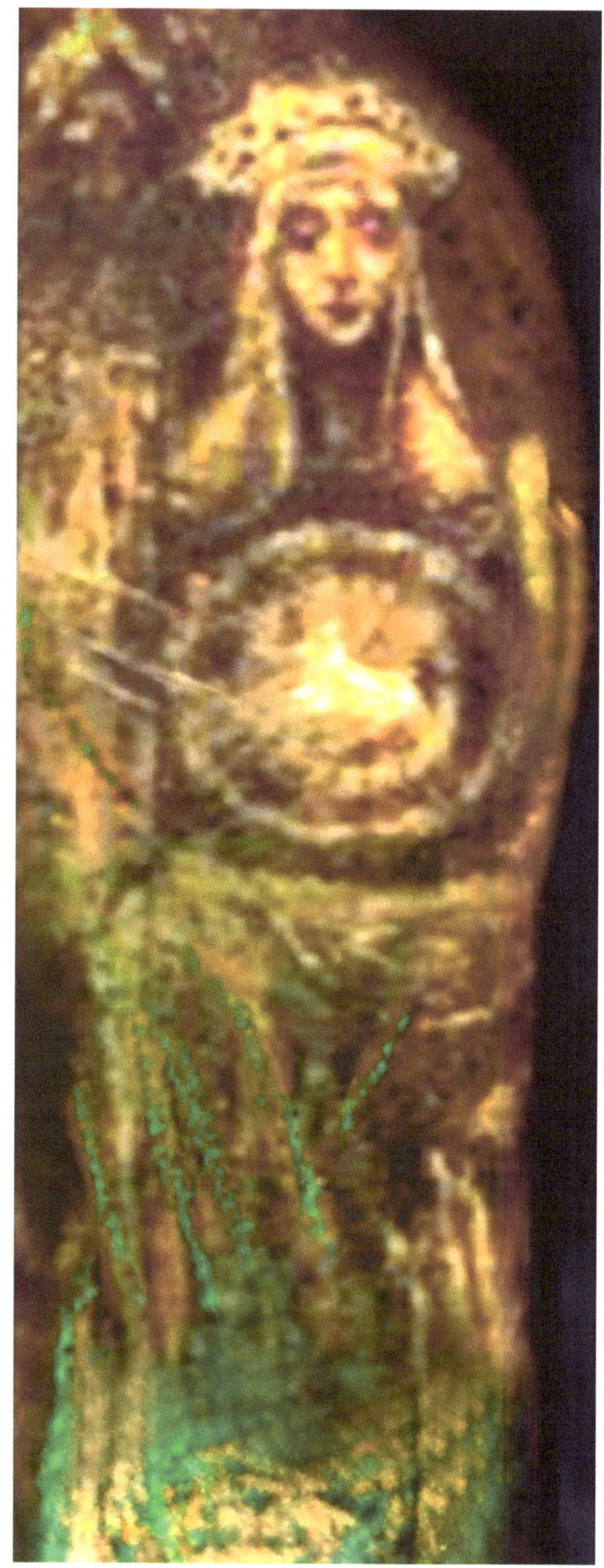

## The Sophia (Spirit-self) figure of the Apocalypse

Prominently placed at the far right side of the overall painting, is an image which is closely linked to a passage in the Book of Revelation (12:1), see illustration 29,

> A great and wondrous sign appeared in heaven: a woman clothed with the sun, with the moon under her feet and a crown of twelve stars on her head.

The painting commences at the far left side, in Atlantean times with Melchizedek, leader of the Sun oracle in Atlantis, and it finishes with this figure, placed at the far right side of the painting. This feminine figure speaks to the viewer about the final outcome of the millennia of activity of the initiates who serve the Christ-impulse: the Spiritual-self arising within spiritualized humanity. The spiritual-sun, the source of the Spiritual-self, is now within the human being. In accordance with the apocalyptic vision, the moon is shown here, underneath the person.

This image is a depiction of a Sophia person, that is, a human being who has developed their Spiritual-self; it is not a goddess. As I explained in *The Lost Zodiac of Rudolf Steiner*, a lack of clarity about this theme easily brings about incorrect ideas based on old religious views, as a study of anthroposophy reveals. For example, Rudolf Steiner taught in regard to this theme that, "Mary, who gave birth to Jesus, had developed the Spirit-self, and **for this reason she was called "Sophia" by the early Christians**".[133] (Emphasis mine) So there was no goddess reposing in the aura of the Virgin Mary; but rather, 'Sophia' means that she had acquired the stage of Spirit-self.

In various lectures, Rudolf Steiner explains why earlier initiates amongst the Greeks, chose the feminine term 'Sophia', and why the initiates amongst the Egyptians, chose the feminine term 'Isis'. The reason is, that such initiates were aware of how cosmic energies streamed into the pure, newly formed Spirit-self; this is a receptive, feminine dynamic. We learn about this for example, in a lecture entitled "Isis and Madonna" where Rudolf Steiner refers to paintings of Mary the mother of Jesus, such as the Sistine Madonna. Of this painting he comments, "Thus we have before us in the Sistine Madonna a picture of the human soul as born out of the spiritual universe".

He explains that these images portray qualities in the higher soul or Spiritual-self, which are similar to those behind the ancient Egyptian Imagination of Isis. He then comments on the receptive quality of Isis or the Spiritual-self (or Sophia), "This Isis, when she has purified and cleansed everything which she has received from the physical world, becomes fertilized from out of the spiritual world and then gives birth to the higher human being."[134]

This same teaching about the receptive or feminine quality of our 'Sophia' or Spirit-self, with regard to in-streaming cosmic spiritual forces, is presented in other lectures. For example in 1907, when Rudolf Steiner was speaking about the famous passage in Goethe's Faust, "The Eternal-feminine leads us onwards", he indicates that this viewpoint is similar to the spiritual wisdom behind the Egyptian term, 'Isis'. He comments that, "The soul is that which is permeated by cosmic dynamics, and it is with these cosmic dynamics that she is united, as if in a marriage".[135]

It is clear that here the term, 'the soul' means the astral body which has been ennobled and spiritualized, and is on its way towards the Spiritual-self. So we learn from these words that, our Spiritual-self is receptive to, and therefore permeated by, spiritual forces, in a feminine, receptive sense. In other words, with the clairvoyance of the Spiritual-self state, the acolyte felt his or her soul receiving the in-raying energies of the cosmos, and this kind of receiving is a feminine dynamic. The main occasion where Rudolf Steiner's words appear to refer to a goddess occurs in his famous lectures, *The Search for the Isis-Sophia*, which refer to the ancient Egyptian perspective. In this context, Rudolf Steiner explains that in Egypt, Isis was depicted at times as a

---

[133] GA 97, p.58.
[134] GA 57, lect. 29 April 1909.
[135] GA 55, 28 Mar. 1907 "Die Seele ist dasjenige, was von den Weltgesetze durchstrahlt wird, und diese Weltgesetze sind es, mit denen sie sich wie in einer Ehe vereinigt."

**personification** of the cosmos, now alive to clairvoyant vision with its many divine beings, nature spirits and general astral-etheric forces,

> Isis is the personified All-wisdom of *our* world...in her true figure, Isis is permeating the entire cosmos...she is that which shines radiantly towards us in many auric colours from the cosmos...[136]

We need to really be clear that the word 'personification' means that a quality or experience is especially presented as if this were a living person. So here Rudolf Steiner means that creation, as experienced by a person developing higher consciousness, takes on a radiant, en-souled quality, and this quality is poetically thought of as a specific entity, a goddess. From these words it is clear that the word 'Sophia' does not refer to a goddess. Rather, Rudolf Steiner is pointing out that the term 'Isis 'refers to the living etheric-astral cosmos, and the reason is that it is precisely this wonderful vista which the Spiritual-self consciousness – called Isis – allows one to perceive. As he taught in 1902, "*That which the Gospels speak of, the 'Holy Spirit', is nothing other than the transformed Isis.*"[137] The Holy Spirit is, as we noted earlier, not a particular goddess, but a term for a variety of divine realities, including the Christ light in the Earth's aura, the new Christ-ed group-soul; the highest of the Angels, and the Spirit-self. In the Hellenistic world, the Greeks, it was Eratosthenes (200BC) and Avienus (AD 350) who decided, in part incorrectly, to identify Sophia with Isis.

In regard to 'anthroposophia', Rudolf Steiner told his audience in 1913, of the need to become aware of this spiritually uplifting result of seeking wisdom, of letting wisdom (in Greek, *Sophia*) really be present in the human soul (in Greek, *anthropos*). In this way a new personification of the soul-quality of the wise person, and also of the beautifully enlivened cosmos, can arise; it is this which the word 'Anthroposophia' expresses. He wanted the audience to really feel a more mature version of the poetic-romantic 'Sophia-Beatrice' idea in regard to the Spiritual-self. He explained that students of anthroposophical wisdom should feel, through the spiritualizing of their consciousness, as if a divine reality envelops their soul when anthroposophical wisdom permeates it.[138] As he explained on another occasion,

> ...anthroposophy is nothing other than that 'Sophia', that is, that consciousness-content or inwardly experienced element of the human soul, which makes a human being fully a human being...it gives a 'Sophia', that is, a certain kind of consciousness to the soul."[139]

Here at the end of the painting, the future human being is depicted, in whom the Spirit-self has developed, and thus the 'Sophia' consciousness arises, to use the language of medieval and Greek mystics. This shall occur in some future time-cycle, as Rudolf Steiner indicated when he commented on the fifth of the so-called 'Apocalyptic Seals',

> The cosmos will have changed greatly by then; in the human being, the Sun power will be present. The power of the sun in the human being will bring forth a sun.[140]

---

[136] Lect. 24th Dec. 1910, in GA 202 p.238.
[137] Archive lecture, 8th Mar. 1902, Berlin.
[138] Berlin 3rd Feb. 1913.
[139] GA 257, 13th Feb. 1923, p.76.
[140] GA 284/5, Lecture of 16th Sept. 1907.

## 30 Archangel Michael

Here the great Archangel is shown conquering over the Dragon. The dragon figure itself is too unclear to see, but it is being held in chains.

## Michael and the Dragon

Finally, underneath this woman is a depiction of the Archangel Michael, who is holding the Dragon in chains (the actual dragon figure is too obscure to be seen clearly); see illustration 30. This is the third occasion in which this mighty Archangel is depicted in the painting. In the modern era, this Archangel strives to help those who seek to develop a sincere spirituality, to overcome the materialistic attitudes which in recent centuries has plagued humanity; and to even advance through to attaining spiritual cognition: that is, clairvoyant higher consciousness.

The activity of this Archangel is a triumphant note on which to finish this, the most esoteric of all paintings inspired by Rudolf Steiner, which was so beautifully painted by Anna May. We mentioned earlier that this great Archangel is depicted three times. Rudolf Steiner spoke extensively about him as is well-known, because he was so closely working with, that is, inspired by, him. Indeed all of anthroposophical wisdom can be viewed as a presentation of what this Archangel taught, in what Rudolf Steiner described as the spiritual School of Michael.

By this term he means that in the spiritual worlds, some centuries before the twentieth century, this Archangel gathered millions of human souls and various spiritual beings around him, and taught them what we now know as anthroposophy. This was done for the purpose of helping those souls, when they began to incarnate in the modern era, to have an inherent feeling for these spiritual truths, and to thereby weaken the power of Ahriman, whose influence is pre-destined to become very powerful in our times.

The first depiction in the painting shows him battling for humanity against Lucifer's influence, about 3,000 BC; the second shows him watching over Jesus at the Crucifixion, and now here he is depicted in his future role as the great Power who has succeeded in enchaining the ahrimanic powers.

Rudolf Steiner explains that Michael, in modern times, is battling for the integrity of what Rudolf Steiner refers to as 'cosmic intelligence', as reflected in us humans. By this term he means the spiritual consciousness or the wisdom of the divine beings, but as reflected in our thinking life, in how we human beings think. Michael seeks to help human beings to think spiritually, and here thinking does not only mean logical intellectual activity; it also means intuitive, holistic higher consciousness, which then leads on to spiritual-clairvoyant consciousness states.

Hence Rudolf Steiner describes this great Power as "the Guardian of cosmic intelligence". Consequently his concern now is, to strive to help the light of wisdom from the divine worlds, or 'spiritual thinking', to live on in our human soul; even though as incarnate people, we are so subject to 'brain-bound' earthly thinking. Consequently, spiritual striving today is helped by Michael in a very substantial way.

# Conclusion

Having completed our contemplation of the Anna May Grail painting, we may find ourselves in awe at the sheer spiritual depth and breadth of what it presents to us. It offers us an invaluable, and indeed unique, opportunity to immerse our soul in a host of artistic images, about some of the most sacred truths revealed by anthroposophical initiation knowledge. By gazing at the Triptych Grail, we experience images that speak to us of the Christ-reality, and of the activity undertaken by divine beings who serve the Christ; and in particular the great initiate Christian Rosencreutz.

It also enriches understanding of many sacred truths about the coming of the cosmic Christ to the Earth, and the role of the spiritual beings and initiates in humanity's evolving. It directs our attention to the role of planetary and zodiacal forces in the human soul. It depicts secrets of the karmic biography of the great Rosicrucian leader, and offers insights into the theme of the Holy Grail.

A central theme of freemasonry, that of the meeting of the Queen of Sheba with king Solomon and Hiram the master builder, is set within the symbolic temple of Solomon. This speaks of the drama of the soul as it approaches the Spiritual-self, contemplating the contrast between the quiet, inner life and the dynamic, active urge towards transforming the world.

We see many Archangels interweaving their impulses in the course of zodiacal ages, assisting the two stern and empowered Principalities. Amidst this vibrant interacting host of divine beings, we see the struggle undertaken by Archangels Michael and Gabriel, and how they are burdened by their dedication to the task of helping humanity.

Through evocative imagery, placed above the crucifixion scene, the threefold human spirit now blossoms forth, because of the deeds of Christ. The Tree of Death has become a Tree of Life, echoing the theme of the two columns depicted in one of the apocalyptic seals.

A powerfully evocative depiction of the unique initiation process that the young acolyte underwent in AD 1250, surrounded by the re-born seven Rishis and others, is set within a Masonic context. This person shall soon reincarnate and become the leader of the Rosicrucian movement.

Below this is an esoteric depiction of perhaps the most sacred teaching in esoteric Christianity: namely that Jesus Christ is the archetype of the future redeemed and spiritualized human being, and his deeds have made such a wonderful future possible.

The more any image is seen, the more powerful is its impact on the soul, since all of our visual impressions live on in our etheric body as vibrant images. If we regularly gaze at this painting, its imagery, inspired from the spiritual worlds, can become ever more a blessing for the soul.

We owe a debt of gratitude to Anna May for faithfully creating this huge painting, we owe a debt of gratitude to Margaretha Hauschka, who decided to make reproductions of the painting available in the 1970's, shortly before she died. Thereby rescuing from oblivion the greatest of all paintings inspired by Rudolf Steiner's initiatory wisdom.

But above all we owe a debt of gratitude to Rudolf Steiner. This painting was brought into the world to help the spiritual seeker understand the redemption offered to humanity by Christ Jesus, to whose divine will, "the disciple whom the Lord loveth", Christian Rosencreutz, has dedicated himself, already for centuries now.

May this book help those who are still interested in making the effort to study and to contemplate such sacred esoteric truths, to understand this painting more deeply, to be enriched and enlivened, to carry on the work of the Rosicrucian impulse.

# Appendix One

## The Description written in 1918 by Anna May, but edited by M. Hauschka

Note: Anna May's description is written as a brief outline; she did place some words in normal brackets ( ), and I have added further explanatory words in italic brackets { }.

Spiritual and physical 'streamings' (the gold of wisdom and the blood) unite to form humanity; within this the great Individualities of earth's history arise, such as Abraham, Isaac, Moses, Buddha, St John the Evangelist, and St. Paul.

The pivotal point of this history of humanity is the Mystery of Golgotha. "Grail" is the word for the human beings, in so far as the person seeks to form a connection to this Golgotha event. The legends say that the Grail {stone} was carved out of the stone which fell from the crown of Lucifer, when Lucifer fell. Solomon received this stone from the Queen of Sheba (left section of the Triptych). Then the Grail became the chalice used in the Last Supper, in this Joseph of Arimathea caught some of the holy blood {of Jesus Christ} (middle section of Triptych).

When this Christ-blood has penetrated into the innermost depths of the Earth, in the far future, then shall the entirely Christ-permeated human being, the Parsifal of the future, awaken out of the Grail chalice, as if out of a sarcophagus and all religions and earlier philosophies be united into a living Christ-knowing. Then also shall Archangel Michael have bound up the dragon, and the Woman of the Apocalypse again carry the sun in herself and have the moon under her feet; that is to say, the Earth shall then have carried away {that is, succeeded in taking into itself} victory over matter.

The upper part of The Triptych Grail presents the spiritual world (gold {colours}); the highest, largest heads: the Time Spirits (*Archai*), who extend out their hands over large epochs, succeeding each other in sequence. Supporting these beings are the Folk-spirits (Archangels). Beneath these beings are the *Angeloi* or Angels, gazing down onto humanity. The lower section that is, of both columns, represent the blood-stream which courses through humanity, and which, in union with the Spiritual (gold {colour}), incarnates those high guides who lead the evolution of humanity. Left, from above to below: Melchizedek, the great Sun-Initiate who brings bread and wine to Abraham; under him Abraham and Isaac, and further below, Jacob and the heavenly ladder. Underneath (left of the cross) Moses in the position as if he were seeing the burning thorn bush. These Individualities are those who are presented here as milestones for the preparation of the bloodstream in the Hebrew people, in order to form the Christ body {the body of Jesus}.

## The Three Parts of the Triptych

Highest middle section above {the} Golgotha {scene}: The Grail – the stone which in the War in Heaven, fell from out of Lucifer's crown.
Left Image: The Queen of Sheba has brought the Grail stone, amongst many other precious items, to King Solomon. Later Christ offered {wine for} the Last Supper from the Grail chalice, and Joseph of Arimathea gathered in it the holy blood of Golgotha, which penetrates the Earth, and which is taken up by 'The Mothers', who are the three earth forces of thinking, feeling and will. With Christ the Sun god, {other} spiritual beings came also down to the Earth, who also work with this blood, so that the blood permeates these three forces and makes them Christ-permeated.

Right Image: shows the awakened esoteric Christianity, as if awakened out of the Grail chalice, the crystalline sarcophagus, and which is inaugurated by Christian Rosencreutz; who is surrounded by {in the right section} the seven holy Rishis, as representatives of the primeval Atlantean planetary Mysteries.

Right and left: linking to these {Rishis} are the representatives of the five post-Atlantean cultural epochs; the old Indian, the old Persian (Zarathustra), the Chaldean-Egyptian (Hermes), the Greco--

Latin (Socrates, Plato, Augustine) and, as representative of our own cultural epoch, the Virgin of Orlean {Joan of Arc}.

Above, left of central section: the greatest Individuality before the Christ-event, Buddha; below him in a blood-column, a pre-Christian initiate with his eyes closed, that is, initiated in a not yet conscious condition.

Above, right of the central section: after the Christ-event: John the Evangelist with the globe of the Earth which signifies: Christ on the cross recommends him to his mother: the Earth. Below this is an initiate with his eyes opened, conscious.

Next to the central section, below right: St. Paul ('not I, but Christ in me') as counterpart to Moses (Ehyeh asher ehyeh – I am the I am).

In the lower blood-course: the Beast enchained by Michael; above this the Woman carrying the sun in herself and having the moon under her feet; that is at the end of the Earth-evolution the solar forces unite with the Earth's forces, that is the Earth will be fully Christ-permeated.

## Appendix Two: more about the name of God spoken to Moses

On the basis of the deepened perspective that the initiation wisdom of anthroposophy gives, it is quite appropriate to consider that the words from God to Moses, could be understood as implying **all of these three tenses**; that is, past, present and future. So such translations as, "I am that I am" or "I will be that I will be" are simplified versions. For the answer to Moses can be understood as saying that this deity's name is, **"I was, am, will be *that* (or *who*) I was, am, will be"**. Before we go deeper into this sacred theme, it is helpful to know that this answer has some similarity to what other divine beings have proclaimed in ancient sacred texts. In ancient Egyptian esoteric wisdom – the culture in which Moses himself was initiated – there are words about a deity who represents the source of the true, higher ego, or Spiritual-self. This deity is called 'Isis'.[141]

Rudolf Steiner points out that in a very high spiritual experience, an ancient Egyptian initiate could encounter Isis as a mysterious, remote deity "on the furthest shore of existence.....from whom warmth and light for the existence of the innermost existence of the human soul, emanates".[142] However, in this original ancient Egyptian usage, Isis not only meant a very remote deity, **it also meant the Spiritual-self of a human being.** As Rudolf Steiner taught, "*Isis is that being which in us goes from one life to the other*".[143] Elsewhere he clarified these words by saying that 'Sophia' meant "*the spiritual-soul in which some of the Spiritual-self was developing*".[144] So Isis was the spirit of the human being and also the remote, lofty divine being from whom this spirit derives.

We should note here that as from the Hellenistic age onwards into medieval times, the term 'Isis' became synonymous with a much lesser spiritual reality, called 'Sophia', which means the Spiritual-soul. So although the Egyptians also used the term Isis in their cosmic way, for these later cultures, it became less profound. It still had the meaning of the spiritual-soul in which some of the Spiritual-self was developing, but this was now less clearly understood. And the associated deity was in effect gone, or lowered to a nebulous feeling of a mystically enlivened, enthralling cosmos.

### Isis and the Self
Now how did Isis name herself in ancient Egypt? The name of Isis, formulated in ancient Egyptian times, has been preserved in Hellenistic Greek by the priest Plutarch:

> I am all: that which has been, that which is, and that which will come into being; (no mortal man has ever lifted my veil).[145]

We can see a similarity here to the words spoken to Moses, but there is a strange and vital difference: this threefold time-expression **is repeated to Moses**. Now, when all three time-states (or tenses) are used, then actually, this means that the deity is **above time** or **beyond the flow time**. So the words of Isis, and the words spoken to Moses, imply that the deity is transcendent over time, and in normal language, we call this state of being, 'eternal'. So the name of the deity speaking to Moses appears to be saying, so far: "**eternal-I** *that* **eternal-I**". But this of course, is not really grammatical, and is therefore still very unclear.

### The eternal "I"
As Hebrew scholars point out in regard to what was said to Moses, the repeat of the words "I was, am and will be" (or "**eternal-I**") is strange. At this point, we need to remind ourselves, that

---

[141] The Egyptians also used this same word to refer to various divine beings who provide the matrix of the Spiritual-self; but as Steiner taught, 'Isis', after the Egyptian epoch, means the Spiritual-self, not a goddess.
[142] In a lecture 5th Feb 1913, in *The Mysteries of the East and of Christianity*, (GA 144).
[143] GA 144, lecture 5.
[144] GA100, p. 243.
[145] Plutarch, ΠΕΡΙ ΙΣΙΔΟΣ ΚΑΙ ΟΣΙΡΙΔΟΣ, cap. 9, p.14: ἐγώ εἰμι πᾶν τὸ γεγονὸς καὶ ὂν καὶ ἐσόμενον καὶ τὸν ἐμὸν πέπλον οὐδείς πω θνητὸς ἀπεκάλυψεν.

Isis did not repeat the time-transcending phrase, it occurs only in the words of God to Moses. Next, we need to consider Rudolf Steiner's deep initiatory wisdom about this famous response, and then we shall actually discover the long-veiled answer to this immense experience of Moses. The phrase here is a very complex Hebrew phrase, because it is communicating about one of the most profound spiritual truths that a divine being has ever communicated to an initiate. However, that is not all. As I pointed out in the *Rudolf Steiner Handbook*, Rudolf Steiner teaches that the human 'ego' or "I" or sense of self is twofold. It is a somewhat illusory, earthly personal ego, in which however is present, either weakly or strongly, the influence of a higher eternal ego, or spiritual element. One could sum up the purpose of the path to self-initiation as, transforming the illusory personality into an eternal Individuality, or higher "I".

So it is understandable that Rudolf Steiner taught that the attainment of a sense of an "I" or a personal ego, is a primary aim of the gods, on humanity's behalf. It is very significant then, that the God who was preparing to guide the Hebrew people in their further destiny announced a name which has the term "I" in it. This is a step for which the Egyptian peoples, and most other ancient peoples, were not ready to move towards. The Hebrews were pioneers, spiritually. Rudolf Steiner taught that it was the strong, if discreet, intention of the old Hebrew spirituality, as it was formulated by Moses into a codified religion, that the Hebrews should gradually sense that in their "I" a divine being-ness, a kind of higher ego, was present.

**The higher ego**
Rudolf Steiner made this point clearer in the way that he formulated the first two of the Ten Commandments, (Exodus 20 and Deut 5: 6-21).   Normally they are given in this form, in most Bibles as,
> **ONE**
> You shall have no other gods before me.
> **TWO**
> You shall not make for yourself an idol in the form of anything in heaven above or on the earth beneath, or in the waters below. You shall not bow down to them or worship them; for I, the LORD your God, am a jealous God, punishing the children for the sin of the fathers  to the third and fourth generation of those who hate me, but showing love to a thousand generations of those who love me and keep my commandments.

But Rudolf Steiner combines these two into a First commandment:

> **ONE**
> I am the Eternal Divine which you sense within your own being. I have led you out of Egypt, wherein you were unable to follow Me within yourself. From henceforth you shall not recognize, as divine higher gods, anything that is a representation to you of something in the heavens or something which is active on the  Earth, or between the heavens and Earth. You shall not worship anything which is lower than the divine within you. For I am the Eternal within you, and I am the ever self-empowering Divine Being.

This way of presenting the Commandments emphasises the view that a primary intention of the religion of the Old Testament was to gently bring about awareness of this deeply esoteric, spiritual truth. This is a truth which the mission of Christ is deeply connected to, as we shall see.

But, we do need to ask ourselves, how is this translation or special way of rendering the Hebrew phrase from Rudolf Steiner to be validated, since no-one else understands it in that way? Certainly his version would be rejected by theologians as incorrect to the Hebrew text.

**Veiled initiation truths in famous texts**
At this point, we need to note briefly that the same objection has been made about Rudolf Steiner's treatment of several other famous ancient texts. One of these is in the prologue to Homer's *Odyssey*, written in Attic Greek, where Rudolf Steiner insists that a sentence there defines this epic work as being about initiation, and not about an adventure story. Another case

is a sentence in the Gospel of St. John (13:18), written in Koine Greek, where Rudolf Steiner insists that this is about the cosmic Christ becoming the indwelling spirit of the Earth, and not (only) about the betrayal of Jesus by Judas.

In both these cases, I have been able to demonstrate that Rudolf Steiner was fully correct in his interpretation of these ancient languages, and the usual academic view is incorrect; we shall return to the sentence in St. John's Gospel later.[146] In regard to the sentence from Homer, academic translations all state something like this,

> He suffered much at sea while trying to **save** his own **life** and to bring his comrades home.

whereas Rudolf Steiner translated the main sentence as,

> And also who endured in pain, so much, in the sea of tormenting suffering,
> striving for **his own soul** and for his friends' home-coming.

Rudolf Steiner then explains that these words tell us that the saga is about the initiate Odysseus striving to attain his own higher soul or spiritual-self. But his version contradicts all known academic versions. However, in my book, *The Hellenistic Mysteries and Christianity,* I was able to establish that Rudolf Steiner's version was entirely correct, even if slightly abridged. Homer's text actually states, if all of its nuances are included,

> And also, within the {soul-}sea, many soul-pains he suffered in his feelings, throughout his passions, to attain <u>that</u> soul, and the home-coming of comrades.

There are other instances where Rudolf Steiner points out that a famous text has another meaning, and often these texts, when read on the veiled esoteric level, are precisely true to the grammar of that language; indeed more correct grammatically than the established translations by academics. So without going too much into the details of Hebrew grammar, how can we validate Rudolf Steiner's interpretation of the words to Moses, and thereby actually feel what the scene in the painting wants to convey to us ? We can confirm that as regards quotations from ancient esoteric texts, Rudolf Steiner's initiate consciousness informs him as to what the text is actually conveying. He will point this out to his audience, and give them the correct translation, in a brief version, to avoid going into the complex details of the grammar. So how can Rudolf Steiner's version be correct here ?

Firstly, we remind ourselves, as Rudolf Steiner pointed out in his book *Theosophy*, the word "I" is the name we give to our own innermost self, our sense of "I". On this basis, he explains that the words of deity to Moses are intended to make us realize that 'God', through Moses, is indicating that we humans do indeed have a sense of "I" and that God is the origin of the higher, spiritual potential in this self. That is: I (God) have an eternal "I" (it is of the past, the now and the future) and the "I" that you human beings sense – in its higher aspect – is also eternal, and is also from me, (God). Thus, I am the 'I am', or, I am *your* innermost self.

But in fact, such an understanding of this phrase does not seem to have ever occurred to scholars of the Judaic-Christian religions; and it would be rejected as incorrect to the grammar. The major reason that they have not viewed the phrase in Rudolf Steiner's way, no doubt is the fact that the word normally translated as "that" or "who" (asher, אֲשֶׁר) is never translated as '**the**' ("I am *the* I am"). Scholars would say that such a translation is simply wrong. But is it really an error ?

**The secret initiatory meaning of "ehyeh asher ehyeh"**
Focussing now on the experience of Moses as depicted in the painting by Anna May and recorded in Exodus, as "**ehyeh asher ehyeh**", or "**I am that/who I am**"; the word 'asher' is an extremely flexible word. Grammar books define it as a 'relative pronoun', so it can have a variety of

---

[146] See my *The Hellenistic Mysteries and Christianity* for these examples.

meanings, such as, 'when', where', or 'so that'. But experts in the use of Hebrew grammar in Scripture, confirm that 'asher', in fact, is **not** a 'relative pronoun'. Historically it has been used in a much more flexible way than that, for it is a word which, correctly defined, is "a general word of relation".[147] What this technical term means is that, it can imply the 'possessive case' (e.g., Peter**'s** apple, or, '*the* apple *of* Peter'). It is used in this way in several places in the Bible, e.g., 1Sam. 13:8: "according **to the** set-time appointed **of** Samuel".[148] This use of 'asher' here would then give the meaning of the words to Moses, that God is speaking,

my name is: "**I am** *of the* **I am**"    (Or the "*I am's I am*")

Or, harmonizing Rudolf Steiner's teaching more precisely to the Hebrew, and understanding the higher "I" of God to be beyond time:

my name is: "**eternal-I** *of the* **I am**"    (or, the **I**'s **eternal-I**)

This valid rendering, disclosed to initiatory understanding, takes us to what Rudolf Steiner taught is the intended meaning, although he avoided the more complex grammatical issues, saying: "**I am** *the* **I am** {of the human being}". So meditation on this phrase results in the following understanding:

Jahve-Christ's name **is** the "**eternal-I** *of the* **(human being's) I** ".

So, summing up, Moses was being told:
"I, God, am the eternal 'I' of **your** "I": the eternal 'I' in which your human sense of self is enveloped, unknown to your earthly ego".

(The phrase could also mean: "**eternal-I** *of the* **eternal-I**", this is probably not meant, since human beings were not then, and are still not conscious today, of an eternal aspect to their "I".)

We can now see that this statement is saying far more than the inscription about the deity Isis revealed. Scholars have pointed out, that grammatically the second occurrence of "I am" is very odd: one could even say, unnecessary. The reason for this second occurrence only really becomes clear when Rudolf Steiner's insights are known.

---

[147] A.B. Davidson, *An Introductory Hebrew Grammar,* p. 47, T & T Clark, Edinburgh, 1936.

[148] 1Sam. 13:8, (*Samuel asher lammowed* לְמוֹעֵד֩ אֲשֶׁ֨ר שְׁמוּאֵ֜ל .) Here it is a 'possessive-case indicator'; it has been used in this manner in the Bible in several places like this.

**Appendix 3: photo from the private Munich Gallery catalogue**
This shows the middle section of the larger 1918 version.

## GLOSSARY of some central anthroposophical terms

aeon: a long evolutionary time. There are seven of these, and we are now in the fourth such epoch. They are called the Saturn, Sun, Moon, Earth (which has two halves, Mars and Mercury) Jupiter, Venus and Vulcan aeons.

Ahriman: an evil entity responsible for the attitude which sees matter as the only thing in creation, denying spiritual reality. It correlates to the Biblical term, Satan.

Angels: spiritual beings who are one aeon ahead of human beings in the evolution; they have the 'Spirit-self' fully developed.

anthroposophy: a Greek word that literally means 'human soul wisdom'. In Rudolf Steiner's usage it means the wisdom that can dawn in a person's consciousness in their spiritual-soul; and which fully manifests when the Spirit-self is developed.

archangels: spiritual beings who are two aeons ahead of human beings in the evolution.

astral body: the soul, seen as an aura around the body.

astral realm: the Soul-world or soul realms, above the ethers, but below the divine, Devachanic realms or true heaven.

astrality: soul energies, but often it refers mainly to the feelings.

BES: the Babylonian Equal-sized Segments zodiac.

Cosmic Christ: the highest of the 'Powers' or sun-gods or Elohim.

Devachan: the true heavens above the Soul-world; a Theosophical term from the Sanskrit, meaning 'realm of the shining gods'; it is the realm of the archetypal Idea, of Plato.

the Double: a term usually referring to the Lower Self.

ego or self or I: the sense of self, but the eternal self is linked to this. Hence the ego is a dual or twofold thing.

egoism or egoistic: not quite the same as the well-known term egotism (which means conceit). Egoism is used by Rudolf Steiner to mean either the state of having a normal earth-centred ego, or for this earthly sense of self behaving in a selfish way.

etheric body: is made of the four ethers and duplicates the physical body's appearance, from which organic matter, such as new cells, are condensed.

ethers: subtle energies which sustain all living things on the Earth. Electricity and magnetism are formed as they decompose.

Group-soul: a spirit-being to whom all the animals of a particular species belong.

intellectual-soul: the rational, logical capacity.

intuitive-soul: (see spiritual-soul)

Imagination, Inspiration, Intuition: Latin words for the three types of clairvoyance, but which mean something different in everyday usage in English to the meanings that Rudolf Steiner gives them.

Imagination: the first stage of clairvoyance: this can be called 'psychic-image consciousness' as it is when astral or etheric images are perceived, (in normal English usually means 'fantasy'.)

Imaginations: astral thought-forms.

Inspiration: this can be called 'cosmic-spiritual consciousness', perceiving or 'breathing in' wisdom, from lower Devachan. (In normal English usually means a strongly felt creative urge or idea.)

Intuition: this can be called a 'high initiation consciousness'. It is a perceiving or inwardly becoming one with another being. This state allows the seer to perceive at an upper Devachan level. (In normal English usually means a semi-psychic awareness of something.)

intuition: can be used by Rudolf Steiner for the above high seership, but can sometimes appear in English anthroposophical texts in its usual English meaning of 'insights' (translating such German words as 'ahnen').

life-force: an alternative term for ether.

life-force organism: the ether body.

Life-spirit: the second aspect of the three-fold human spirit; this is the divinized etheric body, made of Devachanic energies. Is the same as "Buddhi' in theosophical terms.

lower-self: the soul qualities that are tainted with Luciferic or Ahrimanic influences. It can be thought of as threefold, the lower thinking, feeling and will. But Rudolf Steiner also described it as sevenfold, being the lower qualities of the seven classical planets in astrology.

Lucifer: a 'fallen' entity who opposes the intentions of the higher gods, creating an ungrounded, naïve attitude; but who also triggered off the sense of self, in ancient humanity, and who instils a sense of self and enthusiasm for beauty and art, as well as sensuality.

phantom: this term means a spectral, ethereal-physical form which underlies our body; it is not the protoplasm or flesh as such, but a 'form structure' which sustains the body.

sentient-soul: the feelings, emotion (aspect) of the soul.

soul: appears as an aura, and contains the sentient-soul, intellectual-soul and spiritual-soul.

Spirit-human: the third aspect of the three-fold human spirit; the divine forces underlying the physical body, which are present in our subconscious will. Is the same as 'Atman' in theosophical terms.

Spirit-self: the first aspect of the three-fold human spirit; the result of the purified and enlightened threefold soul-body or astral body. Is the same as 'Manas' in theosophical terms.

spiritual-soul: also translated as 'consciousness-soul', and could be called the intuitive soul. This is the soul capacity which underlies intuitive decision-making or intuitive flashes of insight. But it is also the most individualized or 'ego-ic' soul capacity, and can tend towards a hardened self-centredness.

Spiritual-sun: the sun on its soul (or astral) level, behind the physical globe, and also on its actual spiritual level (also referred to as the Devachanic level): these levels comprise many energies and divine beings.

thinking: can be used to mean the exercise of our intelligence, but it is also used to mean any of the three clairvoyant states we can attain.

# Index

Abiff, 15
agape, 52
Age of Pisces, 25
alchemy, 63
Angel, 65
anthroposophia, 106
Archangel Gabriel, 72
Archangel Michael, 71, 108
Ark of the Covenant, 33
armillary sphere, 25
asher, 29, 115
Aum, 22
Babylonian Equal-sized Segments zodiac, 117
Balkis, 14
Baptism in the Jordan, 92, 94
**being whispered to me**, 5
Buddha, 42
burdened Archangels, 72
Cain and Abel, 20
came out of the tombs, 68
castle Karlstejn, 77
chakras, 22, 91
Christ, 44, 64, 65
Christian Rosencreutz, 7, 14, 33, 53, 55, 76-80, 94-95, 99
Christianity, 44
**Christmas**, 78
Christmas-Holy Nights, 78
combating Lucifer, 71
crown of Lucifer, 21
Damascus, 90
diamond, 22
diamond body, 82
dove, 85
dove-like shape, 87
Earth's interior, 51
ehyeh asher ehyeh, 29
El-Elyon, 10
etheric body of Christian Rosencreutz, 95
<u>fear</u>, 65
Feed my sheep, 52
Foundation Stone Meditation, 98
globe with a cross, 42
God, 65
Golgotha hill, 44
*Hamlet*, 77
head-dress, 21

Hellas, 37, 41
Hermes, 83
Heruben papyrus, 88
*higher self*, 22
Hiram was re-born, 14
Holy Grail, 54, 55, 56, 94
holy mystery, 90
Holy of Holies, 21, 22, 23, 55
Homer's *Odyssey*,, 114
Horus, 88
*I am that I am*, 27
I am the 'I am', 115
initiate, 22
*Isenheim Altarpiece*, 47
Isis, 113
**Jachin and Boaz**, 36
Jesus, 44
Jesus Christ, 10, 44, 52, 61, 62, 83, 85, 90, 92, 94, 95, 99, 111
jewel in the lotus, 22, 25
Joan of Arc, 83
John, 19:23, 57
Joseph of Arimathea, 53
Josephus, 20, 23
Lazaros-John, 32, 42, 52
Legend of the Philosophers' Stone, 65
Light-purifier, 10
Lucifer falling, 102
Manichaean psalm, 90
matrass, 63, 66
Matthew's Gospel, 27:51-53, 67
mission of Moses, 30
Moses, 27
Mystery of Golgotha, 47
Nathan-Jesus, 92
Novalis, 41
Ouroboros, 62
Paracelsus, 64
pastoral crook, 14, 20
pentagram, 61
perigee at the winter solstice, 78
personification, 106
Peshitta Bible, 10
phantom, 67
Pharao, 37
Philo of Alexandria, 21
Philosopher's Stone, 65
Plato, 42

Plutarch, 113
*Questions of Bartholomew*, 48
rays of light, 30
replicas, 92
rose-cross, 91
Royal Arch' Masonry, 80
Rudolf Steiner, 46
School of Michael, 108
Second Coming of Christ, 95
seven planets, 91
seven Rishis, 83
son of a widow, 15
Sophia, 113
Sophia person, 105
Soul of the World, 43
spirituality, 91
St. Jerome, 29
St. Paul, 91
stylized lotus flower, 21
Sun Oracle, 10
take up his cross, 43
Take up your cross, 43

Taurean forces, 81, 82
Ten Commandments, 114
tetramorph, 80
Thaddeus Rychter, 7
the "I am", 90
the Cosmos-Spirit, 30
the phantom, 67, 82
the Son of Man, 62
**The Two Columns**, 54
Time-Spirits, 36
tracing board, 80
Tree of Life, 60
two horns, 29
two lines of energy, 33
Urim and Thummin, 20
Vidar, 94
white dove, 85
white lotus, 22
world-cross, 42
Yggdrasil, 49
Zarathustra, 83
zodiac symbols, 101

Illustration acknowledgments (other than sections of the Anna May painting)

1: From the 1912 photo and 1975 poster, M. Hauschka
2: above: courtesy of www.biographien.kulturimpuls.org
   below: Wikimedia.org/ Public Domain Photo credit: Franz Hanfstaengel; Munich Glass Palace, about 1909
3: Courtesy of www.ivanantiques.com. The use of these images does not in any way imply that the ideas in this book are supported by, or are compatible with, those of the owners of these pictures.
4: --
5: --
6: wikimedia.org, credit: User = *Mattes*
7: Painting is in the NSW Art Gallery, Sydney. Photo: the author
8: In the public Domain, credit: User = *Petersond*
9-14: --
15: Above: Public Domain: from Owen Jones, *The Grammar of Ornament* 1856 and late Egyptian palmette column, in the MMA; in the public Domain
   Middle: Public Domain: Tutankhamen mask & statue of Ranefer, from Egypt's Old Kingdom
   Below: Ionic column sketch = wikipedia; 19th cent. engraving
       Marble column = courtesy of the Met Museum
16-21: --
22: Tracing Board: Public Domain, courtesy of the Grandchapter of Washington
23: the author
24: --
25: Public Domain
26-30: --
Appendix 3 (1918 catalogue middle section) courtesy of the bayerische-landesbibliothek-online-de

**Also by this author:**

| | |
|---|---|
| Living a Spiritual Year: Seasonal Festivals in Northern and Southern Hemispheres    1992 | new edition (2016) |
| The Way to the Sacred | (2003) |
| The Foundation Stone Meditation: a new commentary | (2005) |
| Dramatic Anthroposophy: Identification and contextualization of primary features of Rudolf Steiner's anthroposophy. (Ph.D. thesis, Otago University) | (2005) |
| Two Gems from Rudolf Steiner: two archive lectures from 1904 & 1905 | (2014) |
| The Hellenistic Mysteries & Christianity | (2014) |
| Rudolf Steiner Handbook | (2014) |
| Horoscope Handbook - a Rudolf Steiner Approach | (2015) |
| The Meaning of the Goetheanum Windows | (2016) |
| Rudolf Steiner's Lost Zodiac | (2016) |
| Rudolf Steiner on Leonardo's *Last Supper* | (2017) |
| The Vidar Flame Column - its meaning from Rudolf Steiner | (2017) |
| Blessed: Rudolf Steiner on the Beatitudes | (2018) |
| Rudolf Steiner's First Class Verses | (2019) |
| The Soul's Calendar - annotated with Commentary | (2020 |
| The Soul's Calendar - pocket edition | (2020) |
| The Apocalyptic Seals from Rudolf Steiner | (2020) |
| The Mysteries of Ephesos | (2021) |

See also under the pen-name, Damien Pryor:

| | |
|---|---|
| The nature & origin of the Tropical Zodiac | (2011) |
| Stonehenge | (2011) |
| The Externsteine | (2011) |
| Lalibela | (2011) |
| The Great Pyramid & the Sphinx | (2011) |

# www.rudolfsteinerstudies.com

**This website:**

* lists all of my books, with links to some online booksellers

* lists a number of **graphic works especially designed to help in the study of anthroposophy**, and provides a link to the website from which these artworks or esoteric diagrams can be ordered as posters or art prints.

* offers a number of free to download articles about many spiritual themes

* provides a link to purchase my Ph.D. thesis, which was the first thesis, world-wide, to present, explain and contextualize the primary concepts and perspectives of Rudolf Steiner's anthroposophy, for the academic reader.

* has a Donate page where support for this research can be offered.

* has a 'sign-up' link for those who wish to receive my monthly newsletter


It is regularly updated, as new books, articles or graphic works are offered.

To obtain a copy of this painting, see my website, or go to:

**https://www.zazzle.com.au/store/steinerstudiesart/products**

many other art prints or esoteric diagrams are also available there

www.ingramcontent.com/pod-product-compliance
Lightning Source LLC
Chambersburg PA
CBHW060935170426
43194CB00026B/2966